ISBN 0-944094-56-2

Published by
ST Books
ST Media Group International Inc.
407 Gilbert Avenue | Cincinnati, Ohio 45202
P: 513-421-2050 | F: 513-421-6110 | E: books@stmediagroup.com
www.stmediagroup.com/stbooks

Distributed outside the U.S. to the book and art trade by
Collins Design, an Imprint of HarperCollinsPublishers
10 East 53rd Street | New York, NY 10022
www.harpercollins.com

Book design by Kim Pegram, Art Director, *VM+SD*

Book written by Anne DiNardo, Associate Editor, *VM+SD*, and
Alicia Hanson, Freelance Writer (formerly Associate Editor, *VM+SD*)

Book permissions compiled in part by Lauren Mang, Assistant Editor, *VM+SD*

Printed in China
10 9 8 7 6 5 4 3 2 1

Contents

Apparel

For all successful apparel retailers, effective display relies on a combination of elements: lighting, mannequins/forms, interesting signage, interactive and modular fixtures and a complementary materials palette. All these parts must fit together to produce a visually pleasing design that will translate to constant and repeat customer traffic.

On the following pages, we show a range of in-store apparel presentations. Clothing in Andrew Buckler's first flagship store is displayed on nearly 100 feet of continuous serpentine railing. The use of police-interrogation two-way glass adds a calculatedly spooky aura to the atmosphere.

During its transformation of Ms'tique, designers added 10-foot-high wooden display boxes at the front of the store to both frame mannequins and create focal points. Additional visual merchandising displays are placed in a large Mondrian-like cutout display featuring stylishly clothed mannequins.

Barneys tapped architect Jeffrey Hutchison to design its third Tokyo location, this time in the Ginza district. The store has many openings that can be altered at the visual merchandiser's whim. Hutchinson used striking wall treatments and unusual mannequins throughout the space to complete Barneys' signature touch on visual merchandising.

Miss Jackson's

TULSA, OKLA.

Miss Jackson's, known for its fine apparel, accessories, cosmetics and gift collections, opened as a lingerie shop on the balcony of a jewelry store. In 1928, when a 27-story "skyscraper" opened in Tulsa, Miss Jackson's was the first tenant. In 1965, it moved to Utica Square. For its new location, Charles Sparks + Co. was charged with infusing the 34,700-square-foot store with a design that preserved the retailer's history, while updating it with a fresh style. The retailer's antique furniture, chandeliers and artwork were reconditioned and now mix with contemporary lighting, upholstered furniture, stone tile flooring, one-of-a-kind carpets and custom-designed area rugs.

Client | Miss Jackson's, Tulsa, Okla. – Bill Fisher, ceo; Debbie Palazzo, president

Design | Charles Sparks + Co., Westchester, Ill. – Charles Sparks, principal-in-charge; Stan Weisbrod, project manager; Fred Wiedenbeck, director, resource studio; Rachel Mikolajczyk, designer, resource studio

General Contractor | Peevy Construction Co. Inc., Tulsa, Okla.

Fixturing | Oklahoma Fixture Co., Tulsa, Okla.; FADCO, Tulsa, Okla.; Hampton Lane, Los Angeles

Flooring | Surface Group Intl., Barrington, Ill.; Masland Contract Carpets, Chicago; Monterey Carpets, Chicago; Lees-Modivation, Chicago; Ann Sacks, Chicago

Lighting | Lightolier, Fall River, Mass.; Flos, Chicago; Tech Lighting, Chicago

Mannequins/Forms | Adel Rootstein USA Inc., New York

Wallcoverings | D.L. Couch Wallcovering, New Castle, Ind.; Anya Larkin/Decorative Surfaces, Grand Rapids, Mich.; Wolf-Gordon, Chicago; The Design Tex Group, Chicago; Knoll Textiles, Chicago; Donghia, Chicago; Metro Wallcoverings, Chicago; Maharam, Chicago; Callard & Associates, Chicago; Innovations, Chicago; Holly Hunt, Chicago; MDC Wallcoverings, Elk Grove Village, Ill.; Carnegie, Chicago; Hinson, Chicago; Hirschfields, Minneapolis; The J.M. Lynne Co., Chicago

Mosaic Tile | Ann Sacks, Chicago

Fabrics | Kravet, Chicago; Hinson, Chicago; Callard & Associates, Chicago; Donghia, Chicago; Thomas Job, Chicago; Holly Hunt, Chicago; Clarence House, Chicago; Maharam, Chicago; HBF Textiles, Chicago

Furniture | Donghia, Chicago; Barrett Hill, New York; Murray's Ironworks, Chicago; Collard & Associates, Chicago; Thomas Job, Chicago; Thomas Interior Systems, Chicago

Laminates | Lamin-Art, Elk Grove Village, Ill.

Photography | Jon B. Petersen Photography Inc., Tulsa, Okla.

Caché
AVENTURA, FLA.

When Caché updated its women's clothing line and merchandising strategy to appeal to its existing customer base and attract a new, younger shopper, it also needed a new store that would fit its new image.

Designers from Michael Rosenthal created a streamlined, contemporary look starting with a new façade that centers on the mannequin display in the front window. The Caché logo was also updated by replacing the brass finish with stainless steel. An off-white wall paint warms the store environment, while custom-blend woods keep the setting contemporary. Illuminating the new look is a mixture of compact fluorescents and PAR-30 halogen spotlights.

Client | Caché, Aventura, Fla. – Clifford Gray, vp, design and construction; Loretta Turk, project manager; Lisa Decker, vp, marketing/visual merchandising; Laura Haar, visual director

Design | Michael Rosenthal Associates Inc., Miami – Michael Rosenthal, designer; George Galvin, account executive; Paul Gebrian, account executive

General Contractor | John Rogers Inc., Ft. Lauderdale, Fla.

Fixtures | Vision Woodworking, Fridley, Minn.

Flooring | Tech Products, Miami

Furniture | Interra Industries, Keasbey, Pa.

Lighting | Lightolier, Fall River, Mass. (supplied by Capitol Light)

Mannequins/Forms | Patina-V, New York

Signage/Graphics | Granta Sign Co., Stamford, Conn.

Wallcoverings/Materials | Eykon Wallsource, Memphis, Tenn.

Carpet | Atlas Carpet Mills, Los Angeles

Photography | Barry J. Grossman Photography, Ft. Lauderdale, Fla.

Ports 1961
TORONTO

When Ports International was ready to launch a rebirth of its classic and elegantly designed clothing line, it hired II By IV Design Associates to handle the store opening on Toronto's fashionable Bloor Street.

Five bulky columns that break up the sales floor were clad in espresso-stained wood. Space-doubling mirrors framed in stainless steel rest between the columns, while on the wide side of the store, the columns support underlit mannequin platforms. Leather benches, espresso-stained low merchandisers and clear glass tables further add visual interest.

Client | Ports 1961, Toronto

Design | II By IV Design Associates Inc., Toronto – Dan Menchions, partner; Keith Rushbrook, partner; Grace Eng, senior designer

Outside Design Consultant | MCW Consultants Inc., Winnipeg, Man. (mechanical and electrical engineering)

General Contractor/Furniture | ICI Construction, Toronto

Audio/Visual | Sound Dymax Intl.,Mississauga, Ont.

Fixtures | Marlit Canada, Woodbridge, Ont.

Flooring | York, Marble, Toronto; Ciot, Concord, Ont.

Lighting | Lightolier, Etokicoke, Ont.

Wallcoverings/Materials | Evolve Architectural Coatings, Toronto

Photography | David Whittaker, Toronto

lucy

TUCSON, ARIZ.

lucy, a Portland-Ore.-based company with more than a dozen stores, sought a new store concept that would establish itself as a purveyor of stylish athletic wear. The retailer worked with Big Red Rooster to create a "style meets sport" concept.

Using vibrant colors, including shades of orange and green, and oversized graphics, the retailer draws attention to the diversity, individuality and strength of its target shopper. Orange is also used to create an eye-catching storefront. Inside, a simple fixturing system of various woods and stainless steel keeps the focus on the product, which is divided into categories such as workout basics and support.

Client | Lucy Inc., Portland, Ore. – Sue Levin, founder; Beth Zappitello, director of merchandising; Bonnie Choruby, vp, merchandising; Kathleen McNally, director of design

Design | Big Red Rooster, Columbus, Ohio – Aaron Spiess, partner, executive vp; Diane Rambo, senior vp, retail; Dana Fleming, vp, visual merchandising; Dustin Adams, senior communications specialist; Karen Rumora, senior environmental designer; Rich Hennosy, director, production; Tammy Moore, senior communications specialist

Architect | Newman & Wolen Architects, Los Angeles

General Contractor | Boyl & Ames Inc., Portland, Ore.

Fixtures, Furniture, Signage/Graphics | Gallagher Design, Portland, Ore.

Lighting | PDMS, Arlington, Texas

Wallcoverings/Materials | Knoll Textiles, New York

Photography | Michael Norton, Norton Photography, Phoenix, Ariz.

Ms'tique
WOODBURY, NEW YORK

When Rose Rivera, owner of Ms'tique, decided to double the size of her women's apparel boutique, she wanted to take her modestly designed shop and turn it into her dream store. Horst Design Intl. was given the job of transforming her shop.

Starting from the front of the store, 10-foot-high wooden display boxes frame the mannequins in the window. Sweeping arches span the width of the store and culminate into feature display walls. Small jewel-like shimmering metal beads hanging over the cashwrap break up the curved ceiling, while four hanging chrome globes also brighten the area. Additional visual merchandising displays are placed in a large Mondrian-like cutout display featuring stylishly clothed mannequins.

Client | Ms'tique, Woodbury Village Shopping Center, Woodbury, N.Y. – Rose and Felix Rivera, owners

Design/Architecture | Horst Design Intl., Cold Spring Harbor, N.Y. – Douglas Horst, president, principal and project designer; Eric Bress, account executive; John Cajowski, project coordinator; Cynthia Davidson, director of colors and materials; Kenn Butts, project architect

General Contractor | T.J. Construction, Franklin Square, N.Y.

Fixtures/Furniture | Artco Group, Miami

Fixtures | Alpha, Bronx, N.Y.

Flooring | East to West Architectural Products Inc., East Northport, N.Y.

Lighting | Store Lighting Systems, Great Neck, N.Y.

Wallcoverings/Materials | Designtex Group, New York; Innovations, New York

Photography | Chris Lovi/Elliot Fine Photography, New York

Mstique

Aquascutum

LONDON

When the decision was made to give Aquascutum's large landmark store in central London a makeover, fitch: London was appointed to address the task.

Visitors are able to see into the store interior through a large double-height "gem box" window at street level. This gem box features a semi-domestic vignette where clothing is displayed on faceless white mannequins and accessories are given their share of the limelight. Stock is displayed on runner rails in order not to damage the listed fabric. There is also a "silver room" – a corridor turned into a feature room by adding a metal silver-colored parquetry floor and silver padded walls and ceilings.

Client | Aquascutum, London
Design | Aquascutum, London ; fitch: London, London
Fixtures | Cornhill Interiors, London
Lighting | Into Lighting Design, London
Mannequins | Bonaveri, Cento, Italy
Photography | Courtesy of fitch: London, London

Barneys

GINZA, TOKYO

Barneys tapped architect Jeffrey Hutchison to design its third Tokyo location, this time in the Ginza district. The most striking element is a steel sculpture rising approximately 45 feet from the basement level through the ground and then second floor, culminating to a grille in the same style across a faux skylight of silver leaf. The sculpture has elongated peephole voids with detachable wire squiggles that can be altered for panels of seasonal color.

On the main floor, wide coffers are uplit to create the illusion of strips of skylights. Other walls appear to be origami-faceted or have back-lit panels, looking as if they were casually placed adjacent screens.

Client | Barneys New York, New York

Design | Jeffrey Hutchison & Associates, New York

Architect/General Contractor | Garde Co. Ltd., Tokyo

Outside Design Consultants | John-Paul Philippe´, New York (decoratives, sculpture wall, hanging screens and scrims); Johnson Schwinghammer Lighting Consultants Inc., New York (lighting); Marc Albrecht, Long Island City, N.Y. (sculpture wall consultant)

Acrylics | 3form, Salt Lake City

Flooring | Architectural Systems Inc., New York; Studium, New York

Ladder | Putnam Roller Ladder Co. Inc., New York

Lighting | ISPEC, Tokyo

Mannequins/Forms | Goldsmith, New York

Wallcoverings | Phillip Jeffries Ltd., West Caldwell, N.J.

Photography | Takao Ueda, TUCS Photography, Tokyo

Country Road
VARIOUS LOCATIONS

Country Road, celebrated its 30th anniversary with the launch of a new store concept. Lippincott Mercer worked to translate the retailer's statement of modern Australian living into a tactile retail experience.

Louvered pavilion fixtures are used in the men's, women's and housewares areas, with clusters of mannequins sprinkled throughout for additional merchandising displays. Natural materials such as Australian gum-woods, limewashed timbers and concrete floors add to the nature-inspired setting, while site-specific materials, such as bluestone at the Melbourne locations, add a complementary touch.

Client | Country Road, Victoria, Australia
Design | Lippincott Mercer, London
Audio | DMX Music, Sydney
Fixtures, Furniture | S&B Shopfittings, Melbourne, Australia
Flooring | Surface Management Group, Sydney
Lighting | Consulight, Melbourne, Australia
Mannequins/Forms | United Displays, Sydney
Signage/Graphics | Diadem, Sydney
Photography | Courtesy of Lippincott Mercer, London

Joseph Abboud

THE SHOPS AT COLUMBUS CIRCLE, NEW YORK

When JA Apparel Corp. decided to open its first Joseph Abboud store, the design inspiration for the two-level, 6500-square-foot men's boutique, was the product itself.

Natural travertine stone frames the two-story glass storefront, and dark walnut, with a bronze Joseph Abboud logo, is embedded in a horizontal band of travertine.

Ancient travertine stone flooring with a basket-weave pattern adds to the airy atmosphere. One of the first floor's special features is a classically inspired oculus that draws light down while revealing the upper level, where the more formal clothing is found. A floating staircase to the second floor features cantilevered travertine slabs supported by a natural steel and dark walnut enclosed structure.

Client | JA Apparel Corp., New York – Joseph Abboud, chief creative director; Marty Staff, president, ceo

Design/Architecture | James D'Auria Associates, New York – James D'Auria, partner; Douglas McClure, partner; Eric Alto, project architect; Jack Weisberg, designer; Amy Seminski, interior designer

Outside Design Consultants | Johnson Schwinghammer Inc., New York (lighting); Blue Sky Design, New York (structural); Cosentini Associates, New York (HVAC)

General Contractor | Richter + Ratner, New York

Audio/Visual | DMX Music, Los Angeles

Fixtures/Millwork | Goebel Fixture Co., Hutchinson, Minn.

Stone Flooring | Artisan Stone, Deer Park, N.Y.

Wood Flooring | Heywood Burke, New York

Steel Stair Rails | Precision Glass, Maspeth, N.Y.

Furniture | Studium, New York

Lighting | LiteLab, Buffalo, N.Y.

Sconces | Artemus Lighting, Cleveland

Luminescent Ceilings | Barrisol, Kembs, France

Signage/Graphics | Big Apple Sign, New York

Wallcoverings | Donghia, New York

Fabrics | Kravet Fabric, Bethpage, N.Y.

Area Rugs | Odegard, New York

Photography | Paul Warchol, New York

Alfred Angelo Bridal

SAN DIEGO

When Alfred Angelo decided to move from a mail-order business into bricks-and-mortar, the company tapped Cowan & Associates to give it a retail look worthy of a trip down the aisle.

Designers created a custom fixture system that could accommodate the weight and size of wedding gowns. The fixtures are powdercoated with a metallic finish for a soft, feminine touch and feature built-in casework for merchandising and cross promotion, as well as removable lifestyle graphics. The fitting area was placed in a central location within the store. Keeping the experience intimate, however, are podiums surrounded by mirrors that hide individual dressing rooms, which themselves are curtained off.

Client | Alfred Angelo Inc., Delray Beach, Fla. – Vincent Piccione, president; Michelle Piccione, vp; Ivor Hodis, manager, West Coast operations; Linda Pollack, director, merchandising; Joe Welz, vp, finance

Design | Cowan & Associates Inc., Worthington, Ohio; Thomas Morbitzer, design director; Bruce Moody, vp and division manager; Jennifer Crawford, interior designer and design documentation; Stephanie King, interior designer and design documentation; Peter McIntosh, marketing director

General Contractor | The Stone Co., Ramona, Calif.

Ceilings | Armstrong, Lancaster, Pa.

Fabrics | Momentum, Irvine, Calif.; Carnegie, New York

Fixtures | Advanced Fixture Mart, Waukegan, Ill.

Flooring | Fortune Contract Carpet, Dalton, Ga.

Furniture | Loewenstein, Pompano Beach, Fla.

Graphic Production | Alfred Angelo, Delray Beach, Fla.

Lighting | LBL Lighting, Chicago

Laminates | Nevamar, Hampton, S.C.

Mannequins/Forms | Acme Display Co., Los Angeles

Wallcoverings/Paint | Sherwin Williams, Cleveland, Ohio

Signage | Western Sign Systems, San Diego; JC Signs, Tomball, Texas

Photography | Barbara White, Barbara White Architectural Photography, Laguna Beach, Calif.

Buckler
NEW YORK

The 3000-square-foot subterranean space was a former copper smelting factory that had been vacant for over a decade. But instead of denying this gruesome past, designers decided to "embrace the ugliness" and integrate references to the space's Meatpacking District/heavy industrial heritage. They exaggerated the unevenness of the ancient damaged floor, left alone several beaten-up brick walls, used meat hooks to display the jeans by their beltloops and stripped away casements to reveal original cast-iron columns and original Douglas fir beams, now hundreds of years old.

Client | Buckler, New York
Design | ORB Design Group, New York
General Contractor | Castellano Construction, New York
Outside Design Consultant | David Valdez Studio, Los Angeles (metal fabrication)
Fixtures | C&H Steel Iron, New York
Flooring and Furniture | ORB Design Group, New York
Lighting | Bartco Lighting, Huntington Beach, Calif.
Mannequins/Forms | Adel Rootstein Mannequins, New York
Signage/Graphics | ORB Design, New York; Buckler, New York
Wallcoverings and Materials | Nemo, New York ; Timorous Beasties Shop, Glasgow, Scotland
Photography | James T. Murray, New York

Oscar de la Renta
NEW YORK AND MIAMI

With the goal of expanding his namesake brand internationally, Oscar de la Renta started with boutiques on Madison Avenue in Manhattan and Bal Harbour in Miami.

The most distinctive fixtures are from Oscar de la Renta's various furniture lines. Setting the mood from the entrance is a cast-stone dolphin table, topped by an enormous vase large enough to contain a reef's worth of coral-colored branches. Down the center of the store is a high-gloss ivory lacquer "catwalk" series of tables that show off this season's crop of accessories. This series advances to the back of the store, where life-sized models strut the current collection on flat-screen video monitors.

Client | Oscar de la Renta, New York

Design/Architecture | Meyer Davis Studio, New York – Will Meyer, designer; Gray Davis, designer; Sissy Bishop, project manager

Outside Design Consultant | Miles Redd, New York (interior design)

General Contractor | Richter + Ratner Contracting Corp., Maspeth, N.Y.

Furniture | Century Furniture, Hickory, N.C.

Wallcoverings/Materials | Architectural Sculpture and Restorations Inc., New York

Photography | Bill Wisser, Miami

Ellen Tracy
LONG ISLAND, N.Y.

Ellen Tracy's first free-standing store was intended as the prototype for a national roll-out. The company tapped S. Russell Groves to build this first store.

Casual and eveningwear clothing is arranged as if in different rooms of a house, such as a living room or a grand hall. There is also a picture gallery of old ad campaigns framed like family portraits. Textured natural materials are used throughout the store: a focal wall of travertine, bleached rift oak framing the clothing racks and ebony and mahogany fixtures. Burnished bronze and a mixture of shiny and matte surfaces lend a subtle richness to the cream-champagne beige-rich brown palette.

Client | Liz Claiborne Inc., New York

Design | S. Russell Groves, New York – S. Russell Groves, founder

General Contractor | Nelson Construction, Paramus, N.J.

Lighting Consultant | Cooley Monato Studio, New York

MEP Consultant | G.C. Eng, New York

Structural Engineer | Murray Engineering PC, New York

Bath Vanity | Boffi, Milan, Italy

Carpet | Patterson Flynn Martin, New York

Cocktail Tables | DW Woods, Brooklyn, N.Y.; Knoll, New York

Desks/Desk Chairs | Pucci Intl., New York

Drapery | Carnegie, Rockville Centre, N.Y.

Fitting Room Benches | Design Within Reach, San Francisco

Floor Lamps | Nessen, Mamaroneck, N.Y.; Hinson, Long Island City, N.Y.

Flooring | Azrock by Tarkett, Houston; Syracuse Commercial Floors, East Syracuse, N.Y.

Lounge Chairs | Dennis Miller, New York

Metalwork | J.R. Wire, Winnepeg, Man.

Millwork | Builders Furniture, Winnepeg, Man.

Paint | Benjamin Moore, Montvale, N.J.

Pendant Lamps | SRG, New York

Plumbing Fixtures | Dornbacht, Duluth, Ga.

Sofas | Knoll, New York; Holly Hunt, New York

Tile | American Olean, Dallas

Photography | Michael Moran, New York

Laura Petites
TORONTO

Laura Petites (part of Laura Canada) wanted to attract new customers, so it sought a new, spruced-up store environment for its store in Toronto's Yorkdale Shopping Centre.

Since cost was an issue, designers decided to salvage as much as possible from the existing store – including a large part of the existing ceiling, tiled flooring and two fitting room areas – while refinishing and reusing many of the lacquered floor fixtures, wall panels and 95 percent of all of the existing recessed standards.

A new look was then delivered with updated finishes, fixtures and a more efficient lighting design. Designers created a boutique setting using low-sitting metal fixtures, nesting tables, two-way racks and mannequins.

Client | Laura Canada, Laval, Que.
Design | Ruscio Studio, Montreal
Fixturing, Millwork | Ebénisterie Les Boisseuers Inc., Terrebonne, Que.
Graphics, Wallcoverings | Metro Wallcoverings, Montreal
Lighting | Futura Lighting, Ste-Therese, Que.
Mannequins/Forms | DK Display, New York; Patina-V, Rexdale, Ont.
Signage | Media Modul, Laval, Que.
Photography | Carmelo Donato Photography, Dorval, Que.

Billy Reid

HIGHLAND VILLAGE, HOUSTON

Since his debut in 1998, fashion designer William Reid has been garnering attention for his menswear line that mixes Southern style with a dash of urban sophistication. So it only seems fitting that the designer's first retail space carry that same personality. The store concept mixes reclaimed materials and new design elements for a rustic aesthetic with a sense of modern luxury. For instance, custom metal work is mixed with recycled heart pine beams to create display tables and fixtures.

Client | Billy Reid, Houston

Design/Architecture | Droese Raney Architecture Inc., Dallas

General Contractor | Welch Contractors Inc., Kenosha, Wis.

Fixtures | 3 L Designs Inc., Dallas

Flooring | Orr-Reed Wrecking Co., Dallas

Signage and Steel/Metal Fabrications | LM Fabrication, Dallas

Photography | Jud Haggard, Jud Haggard Photography, Houston, Texas

Accessories

Accessories retailers have to be quite creative with their visual merchandising schemes because of the nature of the product. In what's typically a small space, these retailers have to emphasize how accessories can complete a look, add a bit of fun or color or turn an ordinary look into something extraordinary.

Take Bloomingdale's SoHo, for instance. Unlike most of its stores, this one focuses on cosmetics and fashion. And unlike most locations, it does not offer housewares and linens. From cosmetics, to purses, a special fragrance room and a shoe salon, Bloomingdale's SoHo pulled out all the stops for its all-important accessories category.

Cole Haan's first strictly-for-women store was to be devoted to handbags, outerwear, footwear and accessories. Anchoring the front of the store, a modern, tripod-legged display and a white ornate chandelier add a jewel-like quality to the space. The center of the store features interlocking multi-level mannequin platforms for displaying merchandise in a variety of configurations.

For the Louis Vuitton relocation into the old Warner Bros. space, the checkerboard pattern on the store's exterior is also the dominant interior motif: grids and double-square rectangles are integrated throughout the floors, in the checkerboard rugs, the double-square millwork for the product displays and the flashing LED feature wall.

Bloomingdale's

SOHO

Bloomingdale's SoHo store is all about cosmetics, fashion and two cafés. And unlike most locations, it does not offer housewares and linens.

In the cosmetics area, round center islands are designed in white and pale pink, a color created by interior architect Tucci, Segrete & Rosen (TSR). A special fragrance room features a large skylight, one of several in the store, drawing the customer right into the room with a 1940s French ambience. A four-tier custom "Mobile" chandelier shines high above the bottles of fragrances. Throughout the shoe salon on the second floor, ottomans, metal-framed benches and cubes are custom designed, while a woven indoor/outdoor sisal covers two-thirds of the wood floor.

- By Nancy Frick Battaglia

Client | Bloomingdale's/Federated Department Stores, Cincinnati – Jack Hruska, senior vp, store design and visual merchandising; Shan DiNapoli, vp, store planning and design; Diane Koester Sibert, project director; Rudy Javosky, senior vp, design and construction; Bernie Reiss, divisional vp, design and construction; Bob Kapellas, operating vp, construction; Bill Stidum, project manager; Mike Pardee, senior project manager; Glen Withrow, Lance Woodard and John Schlageter, construction managers; Jeff O'Hearn and Elizabeth Grossman, project coordinators, purchasing

Design/Architecture | Tucci, Segrete + Rosen, New York – Evangelo Dascal, president and project director; Edward Calabrese, executive vp, creative director; Lisa Contreras, senior vp, creative resources and development; Marco Oppici, senior project designer; Doug Griffin, project manager

General Contractor | SPACE – Federated Department Stores, Cincinnati

Lighting | Horton Lee Brogden, New York

Architectural/Engineering | Highland Associates, New York

Audio/Visual | Crow's Nest Entertainment, New York

Ceilings | US Gypsum, New York

Fixtures | Monarch Industries, Warren, R.I.; Suss Woodcraft, Montreal; Builders Furniture, Winnepeg, Man.

Flooring | Innovative Marble & Tile, New York

Furniture | Cassina, New York; Barret Hill, New York; Dakota Jackson, New York; Steelcase, New York

Mannequins | Rootstein, New York; Patina-V, City of Industry, Calif.

Photography | Robert Mitra, New York

Louis Vuitton

NEW YORK

For the Louis Vuitton relocation into the old Warner Bros. space, the store planning department wanted to make a statement.

The checkerboard pattern on the store's exterior is also the dominant interior motif: grids and double-square rectangles are integrated throughout the floors, in the checkerboard rugs, the double-square millwork for the product displays and the flashing LED feature wall. This wall climbs from the ground floor up three stories to the top of the retail volume and is visible from outside the store. Other interior highlights include: a wall of vintage trunks hovering above the periphery of the ground floor, dotted with red hat cases and the cantilevered bronze-clad monotube staircase.

Client | Louis Vuitton, Paris – John Mulliken, vp, store planning and development, New York

Design | Peter Marino & Associates, New York – Peter Marino, principal; Maria Wilthew, project manager; Paul Garrett, architect

Architect | The Phillips Group, New York – Vincent Iacobellis, principal; Larry Archer, Doris Almanza-McLean, project architects

Outside Consultants | Jun Aoki & Associates, Tokyo (Façade design); George Sexton Associates, Washington, D.C./New York (interior design); Laszlo-Bodak Engineers, New York (M/E/P design); Severud Associates, New York (structural design); Robert A. Heintges Architects, New York (curtain wall design)

General Contractor | Shawmut Design and Construction, Boston/New York

Armourcoat Plastering | Fresno Decorative Painting, New York

Audio/Visual | Audio Visual Design, Rego Park, N.Y.

Fixtures | Schmidt Tradition, St. Maur Cedex, France; Canus Construction, Edmonton, Alb.

Façade | Josef Gartner & Co., Wan Chai, Hong Kong

Flooring | Fantini Mosaic, Miami; WFI Intl., Delran, N.J.

Carpeting | Edward Fields, New York

Furniture | Cassina, Milan, Italy

Lighting | United Displays, Buckinghamshire, U.K.; Litelab Corp., Buffalo, N.Y.

Signage/Graphics | United Sign, Staten Island, N.Y.

Wallcoverings/Materials | Big Apple, New York

Photography | Jimmy Cohrssen Photography, Paris/Washington, D.C./New York

Cartier

HONOLULU

Cartier wanted its Honolulu store to have the timeless elegance generally associated with the jeweler's reputation. But it also wanted the fixtures to be welcoming and inviting and show off the merchandise. Designed by 4BI and manufactured in Italy, the freestanding cases feature tapered legs, antique bronze finishes and curved, laminated Starphire glass with soft edges. The cases are illuminated with fiberoptics and are equipped with a custom low-voltage Dialock security system. There are readers inside the fixtures, and sales associates are equipped with magnetic wands that have been preprogrammed. The wands automatically unlock the cases – no keys, no noticeable clicks – and the cases are programmed to relock after a specified time.

Client | Cartier SA, Paris
Architect | Barteluce Architects & Associates, New York
General Contractor | Dickenson Cameron, Solona Beach, Calif.
Fixtures | Cassina SpA, Milan; Molteni & Co., Giusssano, Italy; Barteluce Architects & Associates, New York
Photography | Barteluce Architects & Associates, New York

Almacenes Paris
LA FLORIDA, SANTIAGO, CHILE

Almacenes Paris, one of South America's oldest department store retailers, felt it needed to update its store design to further solidify and attract a younger customer base. RYA Design Consultancy was retained to take on this challenge.

At major mall entrances, such as in the cosmetics and fragrance department, the ceiling features suspended translucent arched panels with compact fluorescent light tubes. Colorful lifestyle graphics, some of which are backlit, were also used as a visual beacon to draw customers through the store. The 16-foot-high perimeter walls feature large billboard graphics that function as department or brand identification as well as lifestyle impressions. Product is showcased via simple yet functional modular fixture systems.

Client | Almacenes Paris, Santiago, Chile – Alvaro Valdes, general manager; Maria Pia Rosso, project manager

Design | RYA Design Consultancy, Dallas – Tom Herndon, partner and ceo; Jeff Henderson, senior associate/project director

Photography | Alfredo Gildemeister, Santiago, Chile

Rogers Jewelers

FT. WAYNE, IND.

When Rogers Ltd. asked Design Forum to create a new prototype for its mall-based jewelry stores, it requested a design that would make customers feel more comfortable and relaxed while shopping.

The long, uniform counters were replaced with islands and fixtures of varying heights and styles. The front area of the store, which features gold and silver jewelry, was designed to look like a luxurious dressing room with drapery accents and fixturing that resembles a dresser, complete with drawers. The middle section focuses on gemstones, its fixtures mimicking a jewelry box with trays. Deep gray walls and drapery create a dramatic diamond showcase in the rear third of the store.

Client | Rogers Ltd., Middletown, Ohio – Jeffrey Lazarow, president, Rogers Jewelers; John Brown

Design/Architecture | Design Forum, Dayton, Ohio – Scott Jeffrey, senior vp, design and planning; Brady Harding, vp, project architecture

General Contractor | Fickel Construction Co., Columbus, Ohio

Flooring | Amtico, Atlanta

Ceramic Tile | Casa Dolce Casa, Alpharetta, Ga.; Pantheon by American Olean, Dallas

Fixtures | JMJ Inc., Hastings, Mich.; Avonite, Florence, Ky.; Corian, Wilmington, Del.

Paint Finishes | Benjamin Moore, Montvale, N.J.

Plastic Laminates | Lamin-Art , Schaumburg, Ill.; Advanced Technology, Greensboro, N.C.; Pionite, Auburn, Maine

Fabric Finishes | Maharam, New York; Unika Vaev, Scarborough, Ont.; Fifield, Hingham, Mass.; Accent Draperies, Columbus, Ohio; Garrett Leather, Buffalo, N.Y.

Photography | Jamie Padgett, Padgett & Co., Chicago

Duty Free Shops

OKINAWA, JAPAN

The Duty Free Shops Galleria in Okinawa, Japan features fountains, oversized floral arrangements and softly back-lit columns, intended to sooth the weary traveler. Visitors walk through a glass-enclosed walkway under which water flows gently over black stones. At the end of the distinctly Japanese space, 18 cosmetics brands occupy large dedicated showcase spaces. From there, visitors enter an oval-shaped fragrance room. The assortment of brands is highlighted by a central flat-screen monitor. The main boutique gives 13 luxury brand names their own spaces, designed to their specific requirements. The boutiques, set in a curved formation to maximize visibility, surround a piano bar where shoppers can sip champagne.

Client | DFS Galleria, Okinawa, Japan – David Charles, vp, business development; Graeme Fowler, visual merchandising director; Calvin Chee, group store design manager

Design | RTKL, London – David Gester, vp/director; Hisaya Sugiyama, director; Grace Cheng, principal; Malcolm Berg, principal; Maria Hernandez, principal; Melvin Guieb, associate; Andres Rodriguez, Stephanie Denault, Natsuki Nishino, Takuya Arakawa, Jia Geng, design team

Architect | Kuniken Ltd., Okinawa, Japan

General Contractor | Kokuba-Gumi Co. Ltd., Okinawa, Japan

Outside Design Consultants | Krueger Design Group, Santa Monica, Calif. (merchandise planning); Darra Brakefield, Los Angeles (color and materials); Studio 321, San Francisco (visualization); Immersiv, Los Angeles (visualization); Bob Kaminski, Sherman Oaks, Calif. (visualization); Doug Gordon, London (visualization)

Ceilings | Design Insights Associates Inc., Los Angeles

Fixtures | Yang Ah Kang & Sons Pte. Ltd., Singapore; Kingsman, Singapore

Carpet | Atlas Carpet Mills, Los Angeles

Tile/Store | Daltile, Santa Monica, Calif.; Marazzi Technica Stone Tech, Sunnyvale, Texas; Form Supplies, Singapore; CGM, Chicago; Advan, Tokyo

Vinyl | Lonseal, Carson, Calif.

Lighting | Targetti, Singapore; dform Design, Brooklyn, N.Y.

Wallcoverings/Materials | Yoshiteru & Co. Ltd., Tokyo; Tomita & Co., Tokyo; Maya Romanoff, Chicago

Metal | Chemetal, Easthampton, Mass.; Formica, Cincinnati

Special Materials | Kinon Innovative Surface Design, Hillside, N.J.; 3form, Salt Lake City

Sculpture | Alger Intl., Culver City, Calif.

Photography | DFS Group, Okinawa, Japan

Gander Mountain Footwear Area

NATIONAL ROLLOUT

Gander Mountain's footwear department was set up to accommodate self-service and full-service, confusing both shoppers and Gander staff. Designers from nParallel were brought on board to create a choreography that took the consumer through the natural process of buying shoes.

This process begins at the power wall, where shoes were re-categorized by type of use, such as hiking, casual and hunting, on an existing slatwall display. Bulk stacks in adjacent aisles and endcap displays use the same graphics and fixture treatment, so there's no disconnect between seeing a product on the wall and finding it in the aisles.

Client | Gander Mountain Co., St. Paul, Minn.

Design | nParallel, Minneapolis – Tom Van Hercke, president and chief creative officer; Megan Diamond, executive vp, brand strategy; Shawn King, creative director

Fixtures, Signage/Graphics | nParallel, Minneapolis

Photography | Jamie Padgett, Chicago

Cole Haan

CHARLOTTE, N.C.

Cole Haan's first strictly-for-women store was to be devoted to handbags, outerwear, footwear and accessories.

Anchoring the front of the store, a modern, tripod-legged display and a white ornate chandelier add a jewel-like quality to the space. The center of the store features interlocking multi-level mannequin platforms for displaying merchandise in a variety of configurations. Custom accessory displays, in ivory lacquer with gold-leaf detailing and grasscloth backdrops, are located in the front and rear of the store. Suspended shadowboxes house handbags and other accessories, providing framed areas to highlight the enclosed products.

Client | Cole Haan, New York – Meiling Leung, design director; Scott Fedje, director, image design; Gordon Thompson, executive vp, creative director; Michele Schnitzel, director, retail operations

Design/Architecture | Callison, Seattle – Cindi Kato, director; Chuan Nguyen, associate, project manager; Paul Myers, associate, project architect; Jan Gaylord, associate, interior designer

Outside Design Consultant | Hargis Engineers Inc., Seattle (mechanical/electrical/plumbing)

General Contractor | Herman Stewart, Lanham, Md.

Audio | Muzak, Fort Mill, S.C.

Carpet | Masland Contract Carpet, Seattle

Fixtures | Goebel Fixture Co., Hutchinson, Minn.

Flooring | Wausau Tile Inc., Wausau, Wis.

Furniture | GDM Concepts, Paramount, Calif.; Kaas Tailored, Mukilteo, Wash.

Lighting | Standard Electric, Wilmington, Mass.; Downtown Inc., Los Angeles

Mannequins/Forms | Mondo Mannequins, Hicksville, N.Y.

Signage/Graphics | Colite Intl. Ltd., West Columbia, S.C.

Stone | Innovative Marble and Tile, Hauppauge, N.Y.

Wallcoverings/Materials | Seattle Curtain, Seattle; JF Fabrics Inc., Tonawanda, N.Y.; Rohm Industries, Dallas, N.C.

Photography | Chris Eden, Seattle

Clio Blue
MONTREAL

Paris-based Clio Blue prides itself on strict attention to detail with the designs of its exclusive silver jewelry. So when it came to designing its first Canadian store, the retailer employed similar standards.

Illuminated shelving units and merchandise drawers, installed underneath window boxes, help keep the sales floor open. A contrasting light-colored ceiling and dark Brazilian wood floor create a sense of grounding in the space, which has 16-foot high ceilings. On the back wall, the company's logo becomes a focal point that is visible through the glass storefront, further drawing shoppers inside.

Client | Clio Blue, Montreal
Design | Annie Lacaille, designer, Quebec
Outside Design Consultant | Quartz, Montreal (lighting)
Audio/Visual | Audioshop, Montreal
Lighting | Quartz, Montreal
Signage/Graphics | Clio Blue, Paris
Furniture | MultiModules, Montreal
Flooring | Montreal Parquetry Floors Inc., Montreal
Photography | Yves LeFebvre, Montreal

Specialty

While department stores provide the convenience of one-stop shopping for consumers with multiple needs, specialty retailers offer consumers a variety of specific merchandise. Unlike department stores, specialty retail shops have the unique opportunity to create a brand specific-environment that revolves around the premier product.

For instance, Jonathan Adler presides over a burgeoning empire that sells everything a homeowner with a soft spot for whimsy could desire. Most of his stores, like the newest one on Madison Avenue, are simple in terms of structural interior design, with wall-to-wall seagrass carpeting, manifesto quotes on the walls and accents from his unconventional wallpaper collection.

Elsewhere, to celebrate its Spring Expo at its new Hamburg, Pa., location, Cabela's sought a new signage system for its p-o-p program that would complement its established look and distinctive outdoor brand image.

For decades, Playboy Enterprises has been trying to establish itself as a lifestyle brand through its line of licensed fashion and consumer products. These efforts inspired the design of the 2000-square-foot retail prototype in Las Vegas, which is described as a modern architectural translation of the brand.

Home Depot
NEW YORK

The new Home Depot on West 23rd Street in New York, was a welcomed solution for those Manhattanites seeking one-stop-shopping for their home improvement needs.

The 105,000-square-foot store presents a welcoming façade to the street, with rotating window displays. To the right of the entrance, area rugs are displayed on an 800-pound motorized rack, nicknamed "the spider" for its multiple legs. In the center of the store, above the concierge desk, customers can glance up into a European-looking, multi-story, skylit atrium. Windows festooned with red canopies and flower boxes trailing greenery only enhance the impression that Manhattanites have happened upon a portal into an alternate shopping universe.

Client | Home Depot, Atlanta

Design/Architecture | Greenberg Farrow Architecture, New York

Outside Design Consultants | Howard Rosen Associates, New York (mechanical, electrical and plumbing); U:Lighting, New York (lighting)

General Contractor | IBEX Construction, New York

Flooring | Brominite, New York

Lighting | Cooper Lighting, Atlanta

Photography | ®Paul Rivera,archphoto.com New York

Fortunoff

WHITE PLAINS, N.Y.

The goal for the new Fortunoff store in White Plains, N.Y., a former Saks Fifth Avenue site, was to be appealingly classic and comfortable for the affluent clientele. But it also had to be easy to maintain and reconfigure, with minimal disruptions. And in the 17,000-square-foot department devoted to jewelry, watches, clocks, flatware and hollowware, director of store design, Andrea Fortunoff, wanted to integrate the design with the rest of the store, but needed casework and traffic flow to accommodate the exhaustive merchandise selection.

Designers from GRID/3 Intl. used wood veneers for the department, to provide some color-code demarcation (cherry for frames/hollowware, maple for jewelry). Merchandise categories are clustered around columns clad in a unique combination of a metallic fabric-enmeshed glass over gilding that provides an elegant background shimmer. The floor's core sparkles with diamond cases, while the area is highlighted by brighter white light from metal halide lamps.

Client | Fortunoff, White Plains, N.Y.

Design, Jewelry/Silver/Holloware/Clocks Department | GRID/3 Intl. Inc., New York

General Interior Design | James Harb Architects, New York

Outside Design Consultants | Horton Lees Broden, New York (interior lighting); US Lighting, New York (exterior lighting); Edwards and Zuck, Stamford, Conn. (MEP services); Walker Parking, Boston (parking garage)

General Contractor Interior | Shawmut Design and Construction, Boston

Ceilings | Armstrong World Industries, Lancaster, Pa.

Fixtures | Fred Bauerschmidt and Sons, St. Albans, N.Y.; Metalworks, Corona, N.Y.

Flooring | Armstrong World Industries, Lancaster, Pa.; Innovative Marble and Tile, New York; Interface Flooring, New York; Kristone, Roselle Park, N.Y.; Pyramid Flooring, New York; Walker Zanger Inc., Mount Vernon, N.Y.

Glass | Archetype Frameless Glass Inc., Harrisburg, Pa.; Bendheim Glass, New York; Intercounty Glass, Lindenhurst, N.Y.; McGrory Glass, Aston, Pa.

Lighting | Lido Lighting, Deer Park, Ill.

Mannequins/Forms | Adel Rootstein Mannequins, New York; Universal Display & Design, New York; Rixford Studio, New York; Michael Southgate, New York

Photography | Zbig Jedrus, James Koch Photography, Astoria, N.Y.

Beauty Studio
COLUMBUS, OHIO

Beauty Studio wanted to cater to high-end, spa-only brand names, and chose the high-end Polaris Mall in Columbus, Ohio, as its testing ground.

B&N Industries created an environment to effectively communicate high style and simple elegance to successfully support the sale of higher-priced beauty products. The fixtures were designed to support the sheer volume of merchandise and brands and be flexible enough to accommodate the volatility of brands and products that come and go. Cosmetics tables are strong and linear in design, and rich in wenge wood and white carrara marble. Mid-century modern classic bar stools in a custom dark-brown finish invite customers to sit, try product or experience a cosmetic makeover.

Client | Beauty Studio, Columbus, Ohio
Design | B&N Industries Inc., Burlingame, Calif.
Fixtures | B&N Industries Inc., Burlingame, Calif.
Photography | Michael Skott Photography, Eastsound, Wash.

Jonathan Adler

NEW YORK

Jonathan Adler presides over a burgeoning empire that sells everything a homeowner with a soft spot for whimsy could desire. Choice items: the famous pottery collections; mid-Century, modern-inspired, comfy furniture; lacquer-ware; and platinum glaze piggy banks. Most of his stores, like the newest one on Madison Avenue, are simple in terms of structural interior design, with wall-to-wall seagrass carpeting, manifesto quotes on the walls and accents from his unconventional wallpaper collection.

Not surprisingly, certain location demographics favor certain merchandise. The graphic woolen textiles are more popular in SoHo, the white-on-white pottery more popular at the beach. Platinum glaze is big in SoHo during the holidays but sells everyday uptown.

Client | Jonathan Adler, New York – Leslie Degler, interior designer

Architect | Kevin White, Brooklyn, N.Y.

General Contractor | Prospect Development Corp., Scarsdale, N.J.

Audio/Visual | Bose Corp., Framingham, Mass.

Flooring | Integrity Floor Co., Ridgewood, N.J.

Wallcoverings/Materials | BK Wallcovering, New York

Photography | Courtesy of Jonathan Adler, New York

Playboy Concept Boutique
LAS VEGAS

Playboy Enterprises sought a store concept that was contemporary and sexy and captured the brand's history. Working with WalkerGroup, Playboy debuted its new concept store in The Forum Shops at Caesars in Las Vegas.

Zebrawood evokes the paneling at the Playboy mansion and provides a sharp contrast to the contemporary white lacquer fixturing. The custom checkout counter, comprised of white stone suspended in resin, recalls the famous mansion grotto. A standalone lingerie area evokes the sexiness of the brand with sheer draperies, a chandelier, carpeting and mirrored tile and quilted walls. The iconic Rabbit Head logo is frosted into mirrors or used as the profile of the floor fixturing.

Client | Waikiki Trader Group, Honolulu – Jim Geiger, president; Al Cottral, ceo, cfo; Frank Crowley, vp

Design | WalkerGroup, New York – Jay Valgora, design principal; Miho Koshido, studio director; Craig LaRosa, studio director; Mohamed Gabr, designer; Kasey Watt, graphic designer; Emy Gargiulo, graphic designer

Architect | ids architects inc., Honolulu, Hawaii – Sanford T. Hasegawa, principal; Brian K. Fujiwara, principal architect; Adolph Yago, project manager

Outside Design Consultant | SCA Design, Hendersen, Nev. – Sheldon Colen, principal architect; Vivian Doctora, project coordinator

Fixtures, Furniture, Signage/Graphics, Wallcoverings and Materials | Redwood Interior PTE Ltd., Singapore

General Contractor | Quality Choice Construction, Las Vegas

Flooring | Dal-Tile, Las Vegas

Lighting | RSA Lighting/Cooper Lighting, Chatsworth, Calif.

Mannequins/Forms | Adel Roostein Mannequins, New York

Props/Decoratives | ALU, New York

Signage/Graphics | Sign Express, Las Vegas

Photography | Eric Laignel, New York

REI

PORTLAND, ORE.

REI, the outdoor gear and clothing retail cooperative with more than 2 million members, has long made green design a guiding principle of its store environments. In 2004, its new Portland, Ore., flagship earned a LEED (Leadership in Energy and Environmental Design) gold rating for commercial interiors from the U.S. Green Building Council (USGBC).

The 37,500-square-foot REI store occupies the first two floors of a new mixed-use building in Portland's up-and-coming Pearl District. The retailer used more than just environmentally minded materials to accomplish the LEED standard. The design of the building, natural light and bike racks for employees and customers supported the cause.

Client | REI, Kent, Wash. – Jerry Chevassus, vp, real estate; Peter Emsky, director of design and construction; Laura Rose, architecture and design manager; Cesar de Leon, architectural project manager; Heidi Petersen, design planner; Heather Dale, visual merchandising manager

Design/Architecture | Mithun Architects + Designers + Planners, Seattle – Chris Dixon, director of specifications; Marty McElveen, project designer; Susan McNabb, sustainability designer; Casey Riske, project architect; Julia Stahl, project architect; Steve Swanson, project manager; Paul Wanzer, project director

General Contractor | Howard S. Wright Construction Co., Portland, Ore.

Outside Design Consultants | Hultz/BHU/Cross Engineers, Tacoma, Wash. (electrical and lighting); Sound Mechanical Consulting, Seattle (mechanical); Coughlin Porter Lundeen, Seattle (structural)

Audio/Visual | DMX, Eden Prarie, Minn.

Ceilings | Streimer Sheetmetal Works, Tacoma, Wash. Armstrong, St. Helens, Ore.

Fixtures | REI Construction Shop, Renton, Wash.; DTI, Vacaville, Calif.; M. Lavine Design Workshop, Waite Park, Minn.; Cost of Wisconsin, Jackson, Wis.; Rudy Racks, Plover, Wis.; Rocky Racks, San Diego

Carpet | Masland Contract, Mobile, Ala.

Lighting | Villa Lighting, Saint Louis, Mo.

Mannequins/FormsPhotography | Fusion, Broomfield, Colo.

Interior Signage/GraphicsPhotography | Rainier Industries, Tukwila, Wash.

Photography | Eckert and Eckert, Portland, Ore.

Cabela's

HAMBURG, PA.

To celebrate its Spring Expo at its new Hamburg, Pa., location, Cabela's sought a new signage system for its p-o-p program that would complement the retailer's established look and distinctive outdoor brand image.

To hang vertical and horizontal banners inside the store, Cabela's sought a system that would draw attention to the message, not the signage hardware, and that would not damage the large, vertical rock pillars. A solution was found in the AnoFrameVersaMount™ system from Rose Displays Ltd., which attaches horizontally to the vertical pillar using a strong magnet base. The system caused no damage to the uprights and provided the requested camouflage effect.

Client | Cabela's Retail Corporate, Sidney, Neb.
Signware System | Rose Displays Ltd., Salem, Mass.
Photography | Jack Lerch, Allentown, Pa.

FAO Schwarz
NEW YORK

After successfully emerging from bankruptcy, FAO Schwarz decided to re-image itself as a destination store where everything is an FAO exclusive.

A 16-foot-high frosted box of colored LED light is a beacon from the front of the store. The ceiling twinkles with 20,000 LEDs, programmable for many colors and patterns. Upon entering the store, shoppers encounter FAO's plush jungle of penguins, giraffes, pink poodles and dinosaurs. An FAO Schweetz ice cream soda fountain features thousands of glass marbles hand-set in transparent resin to make up the counter. And it's topped off by frosted globes that morph through a range of pastel LEDs.

Client | FAO Schwarz, New York

Architecture/Interior Design | Rockwell Group, New York – David Rockwell, founder, ceo; David Wilbourne, principal-in-charge; Anthony Deen, project manager; Michael Pierretti; Miguel Petrusek; Jennifer Lordon; Alex Hirsig; Ellen Ho; John Schettino; Craig Byers

Outside Consultants: Focus Lighting, New York (lighting); Ambrosino DePinto & Schmeider, New York (MEP engineers); DeSimone Consulting Engineers, New York (structural engineers); Cini-Little Intl., New York (foodservice consultants); Milrose Consulting, New York (code consultants)

General Contractor | FJ Sciame Construction, New York

Audio/Visual | Scharf Weisberg, New York

Big Piano | Show Motion Inc., South Norwalk, Conn.

Ceilings | Complete Construction, New York

Façades | Showman Fabrications, Long Island City, N.Y.

Fixtures | Complete Millwork Services Inc., Carson City, Calif.; Dane Seibert & Associates, New York; George Goldberg Design Associates, Compton, Calif.; J Glanz Associates, Ho-Ho-Kus, N.J.; Marlite, Dover, Ohio; Matrix Fixtures Inc., Hastings-on-Hudson, N.Y.; MC-2, St. Augustine, Fla.; Michael Andazola Design, New York; New York Fixture Co., New York; Reeve Store Equipment Co., Pico Rivera, Calif.; Salzburg Interiors, Brampton, Ont.; SW Fixtures Inc., Walnut, Calif.; The Stevenson Group, Harwinton, Conn.

Flooring | Pyramid Flooring, New York

Food Consultant | Clark Wolf Co., New York

Furniture | Rockwell Group, New York

Lighting | Dooley Electric, Long Island City, N.Y.

Props, Decoratives, Signage/Graphics | Dane Seibert & Associates, New York

Vertical Transportation | Otis, New York

Photography | Frederick Charles, F. Charles Photography, Dobbs Ferry, N.Y.

The Beauty Lounge
HOUSTON

The Beauty Lounge, located in George Bush Intercontinental Airport in Houston, offers exclusive Lancome, Biotherm, Ralph Lauren, Giorgio Armani, Cacharel, Viktor & Rolf and Palmoa Picasso products to airline travelers.

Designers from Parbel, a subsidiary of the L'Oréal Luxury Product division, sought to create a laboratory of experiences that would draw shoppers in. Display units at varying heights create a rhythm that draws shoppers through the open and airy space. A curving backwall and overhead lighting helps define each brand area.

An architectural "cloud" hangs in the middle of the store to create a more intimate environment. On either end, two smaller clouds with pendant lighting create two focal areas – one for cosmetics and the other for fragrances.

Client | DFASS (Duty Free Air and Ship Supply), Miami
Design | Parbel, L'oreal luxury products division, Miami
Jessica Zapata- merchandising manager North America
Benoit Budin, merchandising department manager
Architect | PGAL, Houston
Outside Design Consultants | Creaction Design Group Inc., Miami
(design and project management)
Audio/Visual | Avicom, Miami
Fixtures, Furniture | Creative Displays, Miami
Flooring | Armstrong, Miami
Props and decoratives | American Plastics, Miami
Signage/Graphics | Color Reflection, Miami
Photography | Dana Hoof, Jupiter, Fla.

Artcraft Collection
RESTON, VA.

Artcraft Collection wanted an eye-catching setting for its one-of-a-kind art, home furnishings and furniture. Inside the 5200-square-foot store, green hour glass-shaped and yellow circular suspended panels hang from a metal-grid ceiling system. Below, jagged orange walls and an undulating purple backdrop provide a colorful setting for the products.

In one area, eight 3-foot diameter ceilings, hung at different heights, cantilever inward from the store windows using a drywall suspension system. On the sales floor, the colorful walls and artistic furniture set the stage for vignettes of artistic wares from more than 450 artisans.

Client | Artcraft Collection, Reston, Va. – Jay Winer, president; Sharyn Winer, vp; Adam Winer, vp

Architect | DRBrasher Inc. (dba Brasher Design), Columbia, Md. – Ron Brasher, principal; Brendan Glass, senior project manager; Sathya Moorthy, project architect

Outside Design Consultant | Micthell & Co. Graphic Design, Potomac, Md. (sign design)

General Contractor | Buch Construction, Laurel, Md.

Ceiling | USG Interiors Inc., a subsidiary of USG Corp., Chicago

Fixtures | Windsor Wood Service, Southampton, Pa.

Signage/Graphics | Engraphix, St. Louis

Wallcoverings | U.S. Gypsum Co., a subsidiary of USG Corp., Chicago

Ceiling system/Wall Installations | Anning Johnson, div. of Anson Industries Inc., Lorton, Va.

Photography | Martin Simon, MHS Images Inc., Crofton, Md.

Caffarena

SANTIAGO, CHILE

Hosiery retailer Caffarena didn't have a consistent store design to help customers identify with the 83-year-old brand. So it hired Droguett A&A to create a new identity that would unify its stores while reinvigorating the company.

Designers began by taking the company's signature logo and white and red corporate colors and using them to create a vibrant store environment. A dramatic red ceiling runs down the center of the 1560-square-foot space. To contrast with the ceiling, the store's perimeter walls were painted white with beech-colored wood framing displays inset into the walls. Large-scale photographs of models and products are placed above each display to identify product offerings.

Client | Caffarena Stores, Santiago, Chile
Design | Droguett A&A Ltda., Santiago, Chile
General Contractor | Noriega & Ricalde Ltda., Santiago, Chile
Audio/Visual | Electro Cabinet, Santiago, Chile
Ceilings, Wallcoverings and Materials | Noriega & Ricalde Ltda., Santiago, Chile
Fixtures/Furniture | Muebles Inventio, Santiago, Chile
Flooring | Budnik, Santiago, Chile
Lighting | Emegesa, Santiago, Chile
Mannequins/Forms | Espacio Comercial, Santiago, Chile
Props/Decoratives | 180 grados, Santiago, Chile
Signage/Graphics | Estudio 3161, Santiago, Chile
Photography | Marcos Mendizabal, Santiago, Chile

Maid of the Mist Store

NIAGARA RESERVATION STATE PARK

After taking a voyage into the mists of Niagara Falls, passengers can visit the Maid of the Mist store on the New York side of the falls, where they can purchase an array of souvenirs to mark their adventure.

A waterfall (smaller than the one visitors just saw) welcomes them at the entrance. Wave-like ceiling shapes and floor patterns also reinforce the aquatic adventure, while the company's signature blue-colored raincoats were inspiration for the wall color. Photographs of boat rides and passengers appear in shadow box fixtures in the store windows and on the walls.

Client | Maid of the Mist Corp., Niagara Falls, N.Y. – Jonathan Schultz, vp, operations; Jacob Sherman, retail manager

Design | SWBR Architects, Rochester, N.Y. – Kathleen Kaminski, design coordinator, SWBR Architects; Rohit Agrawal, designer; Diana Kalvitis-Pannone, designer; Ron Cunningham, technical support

Architect | SWBR Architects, Rochester, N.Y. (interior tenant fit out); Hardy Holzman Pfeifer Associates, New York (building shell)

General Contractor | StoreCrafters Inc., Rochester, N.Y.

Waterfall Feature | iAqua by BluWorld, Orlando

Ceilings | B&N Industries, Burlingame, Calif.; USG Corp., Chicago

Fixtures | Stylmark, Minneapolis; StoreCrafters Inc., Rochester, N.Y.

Hardware | Doug Mockett, Torrance, Calif.

Flooring | General Polymers, Cincinnati

Lighting | Hubbell, Spartanburg, S.C.; Elliptipar, West Haven, Conn.

Signage/Graphics | EMA, Eric Mower and Associates, Buffalo, N.Y.; Traco Manufacturing, Batavia, N.Y.

Wallcoverings/Materials | Marlite, Dover, Ohio

Photography | SWBR, Rochester, N.Y.

Electronics

The electronics market is a tough one to remain competitive in, with technology changing as fast as you can say iPod. With mass-merchandise discounters such as Wal-Mart and Target winning on price, retailers like Tweeter have to emphasize their differences. And for Tweeter that is custom installation services and emphasis on customer service.

Inside Tweeter's new concept store, solution-based (rather than product-based) shopping is the mantra for a fresh environment that, in effect, turns the entire store into a selling tool for Tweeter's staff of "Home Entertainment Experts."

In order to differentiate itself from other office supply stores and to create an environment that was more enjoyable to shop, Office Depot launched the Millennium2 (M2) concept. The vibrant palette of purples, aqua, lime green and bright orange is a marked departure from its former look.

Sprint sought an eye-catching kiosk design to stand out within the 712,000-square-foot Nebraska Furniture Mart in Kansas City. The interactive 17-by-5-foot shop employs a visual communications hierarchy, with plasma screens and a 3-foot cell phone attraction announcing the product.

Sprint

KANSAS CITY, KAN.

Sprint needed a plan so that its small cell phone shop wouldn't get lost within the 712,000-square-foot Nebraska Furniture Mart in Kansas City. So designers from Fitch created a shop presentation based on a large interactive fixture with room for eye-catching graphics that would attract and engage shoppers.

The interactive 17-by-5-foot shop employs a visual communications hierarchy, with plasma screens and a 3-foot cell phone attraction announcing the product. These multimedia displays showcase Sprint's product features and its range of services and plans. Lifestyle photography built into the fixture denotes various product lines.

Client | Sprint Corp., Overland Park, Kan. – Mark Rexroat, director, retail communications; Greg Foster, manager, channel programs, in-store communications; Rick Myers, manager, retail merchandising; Scott Cooper, national account manager, local retail distribution

Design | Fitch, Powell, Ohio – Michael Bills, president; David Hogrefe, senior account director; David Denniston, creative director; Shelly Schnabel, associate creative director; Vince Notareoberto, senior merchandiser/planner; Jackie Pollok, senior strategist; Allyson Morea, account director; Laura Mills, project manager; Elaine Eagle, graphic designer; Benjamin Lamb, print production manager; Jim Penn, implementation manager

Fixtures | Wisconsin Built, Deerfield, Wis.

Graphics | Big Apple Visual Group, New York

Laminates | Lamin-Art, Schaumburg, Ill.; Lumicor, Renton, Wash.

Photography | Mira Kuehnle, Kansas City, Mo.

Suncoast
ALBUQUERQUE, N.M.

The new Suncoast prototype store incorporates both updateable signs and interactive devices into a completely retooled retail environment, created by JGA Inc. At the store entrance, five flat screens are strategically deployed to attract mall shoppers and pull them into the store. The other three screens are suspended in the storefront window within a tilted ellipse frame.

Inside the store, key movie categories are housed in three "feature zones," discrete structures molded from translucent yellow acrylic. These displays run video footage and promotions related to their respective departments. Bright red interactive media sampling stations are deployed around product displays and allow visitors to scan movie packaging.

Client | Musicland Group Inc., Minnetonka, Minn. – Mike Madden, president; Flora Delaney, vp, visual merchandising/store planning; Jean Colehour, visual and space management project manager; Scott Swaebe, creative manager

Design | JGA Inc., Southfield, Mich. – Ken Nisch, chairman; Mike Benincasa, creative director

General Contractor | U.S. Design & Construction Corp., Houston

Construction Manager | Property Restorations of America, Reading, Pa.

Outside Consultants | W.J. Sutherland Engineering, Bloomington, Minn. (mechanical and electrical engineers); Albuquerque Builders, Albuquerque, N.M., (carpentry); Lighting Management Inc., Harriman, N.Y. (lighting)

Floors | General Polymers, Cincinnati

Slatwall | Megawall, Comstock Park, Mich.

Fixtures | Leiden Cabinet, Clinton, Pa.

Ceiling | USG, Chicago

Graphics/Signage | immedia design group, Minneapolis

Laminates | Pionite, Auburn, Maine; Arborite, Elmhurst, Ill.; Laminart, Schaumburg, Ill.

Paint | Sherwin Williams, Cleveland; Benjamin Moore, Montvale, N.H.

Photography | Laszlo Regos Photography, Berkley, Mich.

Time Warner Cable

MILWAUKEE

In order to change the perception of what cable products are all about, Time Warner Cable wanted an experience center for its flagship store and first true retail venture.

The result is an "immersive" multimedia playground, with the company product doubling as both message and media. In this store, the media is the merchandising. A continuous ribbon of 42-inch plasma screens snakes around the ceiling lip about 15 feet overhead, partially circumnavigating the area surrounding the main customer service desk. This 80-foot-long presentation provides a tantalizing cross section of Time Warner's cable programming wares, each screen presenting a separate channel.

Client | Time Warner Inc., New York

Design | Lippincott Mercer, New York

Fixtures, Interior Architectural Metals | Winntech, Kansas City, Mo.

Photography | Courtesy of Winntech, Kansas City, Mo.

Tweeter
SUMMERLIN, NEV.

As consumers become more tech-savvy and electronics become an assumed part of everyone's lifestyle, Tweeter needed a new format to stay competitive. FRCH Design Worldwide was tasked with the redesign.

At the front of the store is a concierge desk, where staff can answer a quick question, set up store tours or give shoppers a map for a self-guided experience. Lining the left side of the store is a series of rooms that suggest a living room, kitchen, bedroom, sports bar, children's room and outdoor area. On display in each area is equipment that seamlessly integrates into such living spaces – from in-wall speakers to TVs that rise from inside bedroom dressers.

Client | Tweeter Home Entertainment Group, Canton, Mass. – Sandy Bloomberg, chairman; Jeff Stone, president, ceo and coo; Mark Richardson, senior vp, marketing; David Rigas, director, retail merchandising; Kate Faucett, director of communications; Beth Konys, marketing director, finance and research; Paul Ryan, director of repositioning and retail prototype development

Design/Architecture | FRCH Design Worldwide, Cincinnati – Christian Davies, vp, design strategy and creative director; Monica Gerhardt, brand strategist, senior account director; Mari Miura, senior interior designer; Cathleen Coleman, interior designer; Santiago Crespo, director, graphic design; Jeff Siegel, director, graphic design; Chad Witzel, senior graphic designer; Rob Rink, senior project architect; Kevin Gallagher, senior team leader Lori Kolthoff, director, resource design

Outside Design Consultants | Retail Masters, Minneapolis

General Contractor | Coastal Pacific, Laguna Hills, Calif.

Audio/Visual | Tweeter Home Entertainment, Las Vegas

Ceilings | Armstrong, Lancaster, Pa.

Fixtures | Dimensions Cabinetry, Orlando

Flooring | Armstrong, Lancaster, Pa.; Bentley Prince Street, Dayton, Ohio; Monterey, Indianapolis

Furniture | Mees Distributors, Cincinnati; Caser Technolito, Cincinnati; TWFCI (The Wholesale Furniture Collection Inc.), Fort Lauderdale, Fla.

Lighting | Lighting Management Inc., Harriman, N.Y.

Signage/Graphics | Harlan, Cincinnati

Wallcoverings/Materials | Architectural Systems Inc., New York; Fashion Wallcoverings, Cleveland; Innovations Wallcoverings, Powell, Ohio; D.L. Couch, Newscastle, Ind.; Wolf Gordon, Lakewood, Ohio; Knoll Textiles, East Greenville, Pa.

Wall Treatments/Fixturing | Feature Presentations, Orlando

Photography | Mark Steele, Mark Steele Photography, Columbus, Ohio

Nokia Experience Center
MULTIPLE MALL LOCATIONS

Nokia wanted to break the current buying paradigm that had cell phone users considering first what minutes plan was right for them before picking out a phone. The result: a mall kiosk-inspired space that gives customers a brand-centric place to make a connection with Nokia products and its brand.

The freestanding, glass-enclosed structure has transparent walls, a perforated ceiling and two entrances. The space marries warm and cool tones with brushed silver finishings, warm wood flooring and colorful graphics. Undulating tables put customers in touch with phones at all angles. Internally illuminated acrylic buttons hold each phone to the table and can be turned 360 degrees, further maximizing the potential of the small space.

Client | Nokia Inc., White Plains, N.Y. – Keith Nowak, media relations manager; Winston Wright, senior marketing manager
Design | Fitch, Powell, Ohio – Lynn Rosenbaum, creative director; Lisa Morales Cook, senior strategist; Randy Miller, director of implementation
Fixtures/Displays | Exhibitgroup Giltspur, Grapevine, Texas
Photography | Brandon King, Fitch, Powell, Ohio

Sears
LAS VEGAS

The new Sears Grand store in Las Vegas was the retailer's effort to reintroduce itself to the consumer. Pavlik Design Team helped Sears develop the concept, which features apparel in the middle of the store, pantry items, like cereal, milk and orange juice and tools and electronics in the back.

There are no interior departmental walls, and the store builds up from the lower apparel fixtures in the front to hard goods along the perimeters. The eye-catching color comes from huge departmental graphics. A 16-foot-wide boulevard aisle runs across the store, with home improvement merchandise on one side, appliances on the other and a 150-foot mega-feature wall of electronics anchoring the center.

Client | Sears, Roebuck & Co., Hoffman Estates, Ill.
Design | Pavlik Design Team, Fort Lauderdale, Fla.
Architect | S.A. Miro Inc., Denver
General Contractor | Big D Construction, Salt Lake City
Flooring | Crossville Tile , Crossville, Tenn.
Walls | Benjamin Moore Paint, Montvale, N.J.; Innovation Wallcovering, New York
Furniture | Steelcase, Grand Rapids, Mich. ; HBF Furniture, Hickory, N.C.; David Edward, Baltimore; Keilhauer, Toronto
Custom Millwork | Quantum Fine Casework, Fort Lauderdale, Fla.
Lighting | Boyd Lighting Co., San Francisco
Photography | Dana Hoff, N. Palm Beach, Fla.

Office Depot
VENICE, FLA.

Office Depot launched the Millennium2 (M2) concept as a way to differentiate itself from other office supply stores, and to create an environment that was more enjoyable to shop and economical to operate and rollout.

The store layout consists of horseshoe-shaped pods located around the perimeter of the store and lower fixtures in an open format in the center of the store. The fun-and-excitement part of Office Depot's new mission comes from a vibrant color palette of purples, aqua, lime green and bright orange, a marked departure from the traditional office supply store look. The new colors also splash up a redesigned graphics program, which favors a wayfinding system over lifestyle graphics.

Client | Office Depot, Delray Beach, Fla. – Rick Lepley, executive vp, North American retail; Joe Jeffries, director, store operations; Chad Mikula, director, North American retail; David Djerf, senior financial and operations analyst; Jay Eisenberg, director, merchandising; Diana Wagner, merchandising team; Thu Nguyen, merchandising team
Design | Miller Zell, Atlanta – Tom Giles, president, retail division
Photography | Courtesy of Office Depot, Delray Beach, Fla.

Windows

Although window shopping isn't what it used to be with smaller visual merchandising budgets and overall waning support at the corporate level, many retailers defy the odds by creating striking window displays that literally stop passersby in their tracks. By combining lights, music, graphics, unique materials, props and decoratives, visual merchandisers create true windows to the soul of retail.

Sony created a layered presentation for its "Technology with Style" campaign. Original photography of Sony products featured items set against modern, stylized backgrounds. The photographic images were applied to the back walls of the windows and then the actual products placed inside the windows added another layer.

Holt Renfrew used a play on scale and miniature wooden mannequins to create a series of lighthearted windows celebrating Father's Day. The miniature figures were manipulated to appear lifelike in such beloved paternal activities as a basketball game, swimming, camping and weight lifting.

And while blowing goodbye kisses to summer, Shreve, Crump & Low's windows drew attention to the small, delicate jewelry products on display. Wire mobiles were hung using thread, appearing suspended in the windows.

Sony Style

NEW YORK, SAN FRANCISCO, CHICAGO

Sony created a layered presentation for its brand-winning "Technology with Style" campaign. Original photography of Sony products taken by New York-based photographer Sara Folden-hauser featured items set against modern, stylized backgrounds. The photographic images were applied to the back walls of the windows and then the actual products placed inside the windows added another layer. Silver spheres and colored plexi rings were added to the windows, while vinyl lettering on the glass, displaying the words "Technology with Style," added the final layer.

Design | Sony Style, New York – Christine Belich, executive creative director; LeighAnn Tischler, visual events manager; Mark Fugarino, graphic designer; Ilana Adams, visual coordinator
Scotchprint Photo Walls | Color Edge Visual, New York
Silver Balls | True Visual, San Francisco
Vinyl Lettering | Sign Solutions, New York
Plexi Circles | Dimensional Lettering, Long Island City, N.Y.
Sony Product Photography | Sara Foldenhauser, New York
Photography | Richard Cadan Photography, New York

Ralph Lauren

NEW YORK

The goal for the "Ski Lodge" window display at the Ralph Lauren Sport store on Madison Avenue in New York, was to reveal the product and the room with a cold afternoon sensibility.

To achieve that objective, designer Shelly Sabel used key and fill light effects and a series of light-blocking screens, spread lenses and daylight filters. The result was a clear, crisp mood and setting that is inherently consistent with the products on display.

Client | Ralph Lauren, New York
Design | Shelly Sabel, New York; Eric Warner, New York
Lighting | Lighting Services Inc (LSI), Stony Point, N.Y.
Photography | Courtesy of Polo Ralph Lauren, Nantucket, Mass.

Marshall Field's / 40th Anniversary of the Chicago International Film Fesitval

CHICAGO

To highlight the 40th anniversary of the Chicago International Film Festival, Marshall Field's took inspiration from the event's promotional poster, which used several tiny photos to create one large image, to fashion a window display for its State Street flagship.

Festival posters were layered in rows to simulate film strips that ran down the walls and continued onto the floor. A mannequin donned a dress made entirely of film fest T-shirts, banners and actual film strips while tipping her black derby hat to hanging images of honorees Faye Dunaway and Sigourney Weaver.

Design | Marshall Field's, Chicago – Jamie Becker, creative director; Amy Meadows, visual marketing manager; State Street Window Display Staff
Photography | Susan Kezon, Chicago

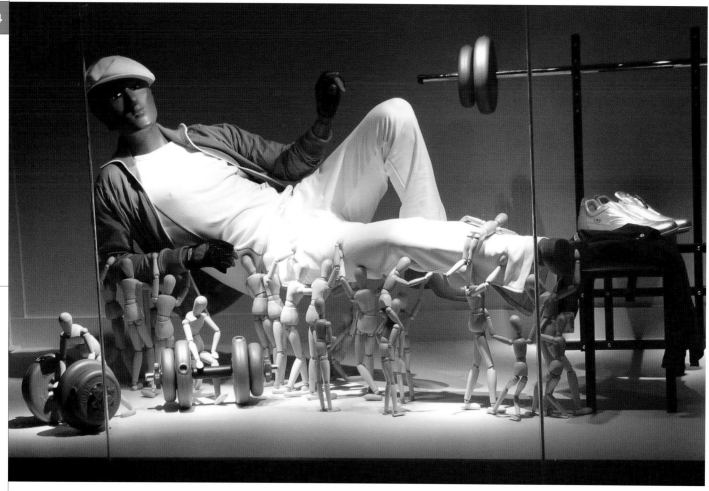

Holt Renfrew

TORONTO

Taking inspiration from the Lilliputian segment of *Gulliver's Travels*, Holt Renfrew used a play on scale and miniature wooden mannequins to create a series of lighthearted windows celebrating Father's Day.

The miniature figures were manipulated to appear lifelike in such beloved paternal activities as a basketball game, swimming, camping and weight lifting. In the basketball scene, a player is challenged by four wooden dolls. Additional propping, such as using pairs of shoes as the flames of the campfire and assorted jeans for the waves of the swimming pool, further added to the creative spirit of the windows.

Design | Holt Renfrew, Toronto – Janis Bell, former national visual director; Mary Pompili, vp, marketing; Daniel Giles, former creative director; Tracey Peters, national visual merchandising manager; Suzanne Shaw, visual manager

Mannequins/Forms | Pucci Intl., New York; DK Display, New York

Signage/Graphics, Vinyl | Dot and Dash, Toronto

Photography | Jay Robis, Saw Photography, Toronto

Father's Day
June 20th

Shreve, Crump & Low

BOSTON

The goal for Shreve, Crump & Low's "Fall 2004/Kisses" windows was to catch shoppers' eyes while drawing attention to the small, delicate jewelry products on display. Wire mobiles were hung using thread, appearing suspended in the windows. While blowing goodbye kisses to summer, the retailer's bejeweled items also appeared to be blowing in the wind. With the use of dramatic lighting, the window displays captured the "blue" emotion of saying goodbye to summer, with a twist of elegance in bringing in the fall season.

Client | Shreve, Crump & Low, Boston
Design | Sightgeist Design, Boston – Lucy-Ann Bouwman, visual display director; Jonathan Ro-Schofield, Patrick Scales, Christina Zwart, design team
Lighting | Lighting Services Inc, Stony Point, N.Y.
Props/Decoratives | Sightgeist Design, Boston
Photography | Chris Akelian, Boston

Marshall Field's / JLO Lingere

CHICAGO

To celebrate the launch of Jennifer Lopez's lingerie line, Marshall Field's fashioned a peek-a-boo style window display that highlighted the product while calling attention to Lopez's rising brand status.

An enlarged JLO logo was painted onto the window glass, leaving only the letters transparent. Passersby had to peek inside to see the product line modeled on realistic mannequins. Lighting in shades of pink and peach added a warm, feminine touch.

Design | Marshall Field's, Chicago – Jamie Becker, creative director; Amy Meadows, visual marketing manager; State Street Window Display Staff

Photography | Susan Kezon, Chicago

Shreve, Crump & Low

BOSTON

Shreve, Crump & Low's "4th of July Bicycles" windows defied the aperture of the small jewelry-box window opening by using parts of full-size bicycles. Designer Lucy-Ann Bouwman used track-mounted 216 Series (MR-16) lamps and color filters in light blue, straw and flesh pink to give the illusion of a large space within a jewelry environment. The lighting gave the illusion of movement to the mechanics of a bicycle, while narrow spotlighting provided even more drama.

Client | Shreve, Crump & Low, Boston
Design | Sightgeist Design, Boston
Lucy-Ann Bouwman, visual display director
Lighting | Lighting Services Inc, Stony Point, N.Y.
Photography | Chris Akelian, Boston

Timberland's Travel Gear In-Store Launch

MULTIPLE LOCATIONS

Timberland needed an attention-grabbing window display to announce the launch of its Travel Gear footwear line, which features interchangeable components that allows travelers to adapt their footwear to their clothing or travel environment.

Supporting the premise of the line, "Pack Less, Do More," the multi-part window display featured an airline route map, bustform and luggage. Footwear and product feature/benefit graphics suggested an end use -- business, touring and adventure.

Design | The Timberland Co., Stratham, N.H. – Bevan Bloemendaal, senior director, global creative services; David Curtis, senior manager, environments group; Jean Wood, fixturing manager; Victoria Dimou, director, art and copy; Susan Emerick, project manager; Amy Tauchert, visual merchandising

Fixtures, Signage/Graphics | The Royal Promotion Group, New York; Benchmark, Cincinnati

Signage/Graphics | Synnott Imaging, Plainfield, Conn.

Photography | Mark Steele Photography, Columbus

Holt Renfrew
TORONTO

Holt Renfrew created the "Vinyl – Style in the Groove" multifaceted retail marketing campaign for its Canadian department stores.

Along Bloor Street, window displays played on the glamour and fashion of the rock-and-roll lifestyle, including mirrored curtains and references to musical legends like The Doors. Inside, each floor of the store centered on a different music genre, including Hip Hop, House and Underground. Fashion displays and visuals played back to that theme through propping, including pink ceiling trim, deejay tables and mannequin styling, while photographs by Allison Jackson of singers' look-alikes, including Cher, elevated the star appeal.

Design | Holt Renfrew, Toronto – Janis Bell, former national visual director; Mary Pompili, vp, marketing; Daniel, director, former creative services; Gwen Gibson, director, national special events; Janet Eger, director, communications; Tracey Peters, national visual merchandising manager; Susanne Shaw, visual manager

Outside Design Consultants | Allison Koturbash, Toronto (set designer); Little Feet Ltd., Toronto (scenery, display and manufacturing); Concrete Design, Toronto (icon designers); Dot and Dash, Toronto (props and decoratives, vinyl); BGM Imaging, Toronto (surfaces, display, icons); Westbury National Show Systems Ltd., Toronto (lighting)

Mannequins/Forms | Adel Rootstein Mannequins, London
Photography | Jay Robis, Saw Photography, Toronto

Saks Fifth Avenue

NEW YORK

Saks Fifth Avenue's "St. John Newspaper Heiress" display highlights St. John fashion with a heavenly realm of newspapers in a cool moody blue scene. Lighting designer James Ransom used 200 Series (PAR46) and 30 Series low-voltage (PAR46) fixtures and glass filters, including medium blue, daylight and "Gene Moore Blue." The result: a dramatic but austere environment.

Client | Saks Fifth Avenue, New York – James Ranson, lighting designer
Lighting | Lighting Services Inc, Stony Point, N.Y.
Photography | Michael Ross, New York

Food

Food retailers fight an ongoing battle to distinguish them-selves in a highly competitive market. Price, freshness, variety, selection and brands have always been among the weapons of choice. But so, increasingly, is store layout and merchandising, as designers take cues from the retailer's premier product, using color and design schemes that en-hance rather than overwhelm the quality of the food.

To counter skyrocketing energy costs, Stop & Shop devel-oped the Low Energy Super Store by replacing all of its exist-ing metal halide downlights with T5 fluorescents. Special consideration was taken both to enhance color and to avoid food spoilage.

When DELICA rf-1 decided to expand outside of Japan, San Francisco seemed like a winning location for its first U.S.-based gourmet delicatessen. A sharing table for in-store dining supports the open and warm mood, which offers fresh salads and foods prepared and displayed in the open.

Real Canadian Superstore opened one of its largest stores in Toronto, consisting of everything from a dry cleaner to a medical center and a shoe repair kiosk. For the growing percentage of households less interested in cooking five nights a week, a Meals to Go area offers quick and nutritious meal solutions.

Fry's Marketplace
CHANDLER, ARIZ.

The Kroger Co. sought a new formula for combining grocery and general merchandise into one store format. The lifestyle store, named Fry's Marketplace, features three key components – a neighborhood organizational layout, lifestyle vignettes and merchandise-forward signage.

The store's five neighborhoods are Fresh, Value, Home, Health and Occasion. Each department has its own distinctive color and materials palette, decor and background music. In the celebration area – where toys, snacks, cards, gifts and flowers are sold – designers suspended a large card rack with balloons and streamers trailing off over the department. Chandeliers comprised of teapots and coffee spoons hang above the coffee and tea area.

Client | The Kroger Co., Cincinnati – Ken Pray, coordinator of store design; Mary Gawle, interior store design
Fry's Food Stores of AZ, Tolleson, Ariz. – Michael Donnelly, president; Steven Hagen, director, facility engineering

Design | Shook Kelley, Los Angeles – Kevin Kelley, lead principal/brand strategy; Stan Rostas, Frank Quattrocchi, Mike Nicholls, Kevin O'Donnell, Kevin Kennedy, Terry Vickers, Linda Krause, designer/architects; Todd Roland, environmental designer; Rosalind Doty, designer

Architect | Kurt D. Reed Associates Inc., Scottsdale, Ariz.

Decor Fabrication | Schorleaf Inc., Phoenix

Flooring | L.M. Scofield Co., Los Angeles

Wall/Floor Tile | Dal-Tile Corp., Dallas

Decorative Wall Finish | Triarch Industries, Houston

Cork Panels | Jelinek Group, Oakville, Ont.

Paint | Frazee, San Diego; Benjamin Moore & Co., Montvale, N.J.; Pratt & Lambert, Cleveland; Pittsburgh Paints, Pittsburgh

Laminates | Pionite, Auburn, Maine; Wilsonart Intl., Temple, Texas; Nevamar Co., Odenton, Md.; Formica, Cincinnati

Vinyl Film | 3M, St. Paul, Minn.

Refrigerated Cases, Shelving | Hussmann Corp, Bridgeton, Mo.; Madix Store Fixtures, Goodwater, Ala.

Stop & Shop
MULTIPLE LOCATIONS

To counter skyrocketing energy costs, Stop & Shop developed the "Low Energy Super Store," or LESS project.

The supermarket's existing metal halide downlights were replaced with T5 fluorescents. Ambient light is supplied throughout the store by more than 50 skylights that enhance the colors and quality of the environment. To keep direct sunlight from damaging products in areas like produce, a special glazing film filters UV and other harmful rays, while reflectors redirect the light to bounce off the ceiling before hitting the products. And 39-watt metal halide spotlights highlight endcap displays, product spotlights and in-store signage.

Client | Stop & Shop, Quincy, Mass.

Design | Group Red LLC, New York

Architect | Carter & Burgess, Cambridge, Mass.

Outside Design Consultants | Clanton & Associates, Boulder, Colo. (lighting); ENSAR Group, Boulder, Colo. (daylighting consultants); Fore Solutions, Portland, Maine (sustainability consultants); Rocky Mountain Institute (RMI), Snowmass, Colo. (resource-efficient business solution)

General Contractor | Bowdoin Construction Corp., Needham Heights, Mass.

Lighting | Philips Lighting Co., Somerset, N.J.; Lighting Services Inc., Stony Point, N.Y.

Dimming System | Lutron Electronics Co., Coopersburg, Pa.

Glazing Film | 3M Co., St. Paul, Minn.

Photography | Paul Horwitz, Atlantic Photo, Boston

Jimmy Buffett's Margaritaville
LAS VEGAS

Designers for Jimmy Buffett's Margaritaville restaurant on the Las Vegas strip, wanted to create a place that authentically imbued the Buffett lifestyle. A "live" volcano rests in the middle of the restaurant. One volcano show uses sound effects coupled with a Jimmy Buffett video and the down-pouring of green margarita mix. The restaurant's booths resemble boats, adding to the island theme. A scaled model plane is featured overhead with working props. The plane is illuminated with a number of focused fixtures at all angles to avoid becoming an obstruction to the dance floor and dining tables.

Client | Caesars Entertainment, Las Vegas; Margaritaville Holdings, Palm Beach, Fla.

Design | The McBride Co., Miami – Patrick McBride, ceo; Eric McBride, president; Terry Guilbeau, project designer

Architect | TSA Nevada, Las Vegas – Mark Zwagerman

Lighting and Multi-Media Design and Implementation | Illuminating Concepts, Farmington Hills, Mich. – Ron Harwood, creative director; Mark Borus, project design manager; Michael Shulman, project manager; John Bartley, controls & dimming; Scott Stephens, control systems design and creative programming

General Contractor | Penta Building Group, Las Vegas

Mechanical Engineer | Hanson, Springfield, Ill.

Audio/Visual | JBL Audio, Northridge, Calif.; Crown Audio, Elkhart, Ind.; Sanyo, Chatsworth, Calif.

Painted Ceilings and Murals | Oatis Design Alliance, Denver

Flooring | Arcon Intl., Las Vegas

Lighting | Martin Professional, Sunrise, Fla.; Indy Lighting, Fishers, Ind.; Capri Lighting, Atlanta; Rab Lighting, Northvale, N.J.; West Marine, Watsonville, Calif.

Props/Decoratives | George M. Raymond Co., Orange, Calif.; Trans Forms, Montreal; Commercial Cabinets, Las Vegas

Signage/Graphics | The McBride Co., Miami – Brenda Grady, graphic designer

Photography | Ron Harwood & Scott Stephens, Illuminating Concepts, Farmington Hills, Mich.

Real Canadian Superstore

TORONTO

The 150,000-square-foot Real Canadian Superstore is one of the banner's largest. Consisting of two levels, it encompasses three major categories: fresh foods, health and beauty, and home and lifestyle, each color-coded to help shoppers navigate the space with ease.

The lower galleria offers a photo studio, optical center, medical clinic, bank, shoe repair kiosk, dry cleaner and florist. The upper level features a convenient Meals to Go area, as well as a cooking school, fitness center and drugstore. This level also boasts a large home décor section, as well as apparel and fitting rooms.

A bright and crisp color palette, promotional signage and oversized photography create visual interest and further facilitate wayfinding.

Client | Real Canadian Superstore, Toronto – Joe Jackman, executive vp, marketing; Fred Dumais, senior vp, supermarket development and construction; Paul Mumford, senior director, retail development; Mark Lis, senior director, Superstore/Zehrs/Loblaw/Fortino's; Mike Farquhar, senior director, store merchandising and development; Almira Peadzic, manager, retail décor and signage

Design | Perennial Inc., Toronto – Tara O'Neil, director of design, environments; Cindy Yealland, senior designer, environments; Kimberly Wickham, junior designer, environments; Brent Roth, design director; Mike Kazalac, intermediate designer, creative; Paul Cronin, intermediate deisgner, creative; Sandra Messore-Duff, business director; Patty Austin, business manager; Jim King, executive vp, co-chief creative officer

Architect | Sweeny Sterling Finlayson & Co. Architects Inc., Toronto

Outside Design Consultant | Hammerschlau & Joffe, Toronto (lighting, engineering and graphics)

General Contractor | Carwell Construction, Toronto

Fixtures | Display Fixtures, Winnipeg, Man.; Lozier Fixtures, Grand Island, N.Y.; Shaw Woodworks Inc., Collingwood, Ont.

Flooring | Centura Tiles, Toronto

Furniture | ISA, Toronto

Lighting | Lightolier, Toronto

Props/Decoratives | Food Supplies Distributing, Concord, Ont.

Signage/Graphics | Ad Display, Quebec; Sommerville Merchandising, Toronto; Panigas, Toronto

Flooring | Savoia Canada, Toronto; GE Shnier Co., Toronto

Photography | Richard Johnson, Toronto

Lindt Master Chocolatier

FREEHOLD, N.J.

Swiss chocolatier Lindt & Sprungli sought a new prototype that would express its European mastery of fine chocolate-making to a North American audience.

Designers at JGA Inc. found a solution in a delicate selection of textures and artisan materials that mixed Olde World with today. For instance, a contemporary storefront – an internally illuminated glass frame with an oversized image of a maitre d'chocolat, glass mosaics and bronze metallic signage – is juxtaposed with hand-forged metals and wrought iron display elements inside the store. Chocolate brown bookshelves align the perimeter wall, while a focal market table display – featuring wood and tiled tables and iron pot racks hanging above – suggests a gourmet kitchen.

Client | Lindt & Sprungli, Stratham, N.H. – Scott Jackson, vp, retail operations; Michael Weeks, director, store planning and real estate; Kim MacLaren, construction manager

Design | JGA Inc., Southfield, Mich. – Ken Nisch, chairman; Kathi McWilliams, creative director; Mike McCahill, project manager

Architect | Aedifica Inc., Montreal

General Contractor | JH Construction, Newark, Del.

Flooring | Virginia Tile Co., Farmington Hills, Mich.

Fixtures/Furniture | Golden Oldies, Flushing, N.Y.; Look, New York

Ceiling | Contract Options, Grosse Pointe Woods, Mich.

Audio/Visual | DMX, Northboro, Mass.; install@FX, Boston

Props/Decoratives | Van Stry Design, Malden, Mass.; Planteriors, Berkeley Heights, N.J.; Viaggio Inc., Farmingdale, N.Y.; Martin Aborn/Richard Cohen, Hingham, Mass.

Signage/Graphics | Advanced Photographics, Danvers, Mass.; JS McCarthy Printing, Augusta, Maine; Color Associates, St. Louis; Triangle Sign, Baltimore

Lighting | Lighting Management Inc., Harriman, N.Y.

Photography | Kevin Brusie Photography, Portland, Maine

DELICA rf-1
SAN FRANCISCO

When Rockfield Co. began looking to expand outside Japan, it was drawn to San Francisco, known for its abundance of fresh artisan food and local producers.

The new location, called DELICA rf-1, is a 2000-square-foot gourmet delicatessen in San Francisco's Ferry Building Marketplace. CCS Architecture adapted the brand to the U.S. audience using a sensuous, minimalist environment of light woods and stainless-steel accents. A sharing table for in-store dining supports the open and warm mood, which offers fresh salads and foods prepared and displayed in the open. Kitchen zones provide visual excitement, with prepared foods taking the foreground, while the processed and raw products provide an essential backdrop.

Client | Rockfield Co. Ltd., Kobe, Japan
Design/Architecture | CCS Architecture, San Francisco
Outside Design Consultants | Revolver Design, Emeryville, Calif. (lighting); Yagi Design, San Francisco (graphics); Federighi Food Machinery, San Francisco (food service)
Audio/Visual | Pro Media, Hercules, Calif.
Chairs | Arkitektura, San Francisco
Lighting | Revolver Design, Emeryville, Calif.
Signage/Graphics | Yagi Design, San Francisco
Photography | Cesar Rubio Photography, San Francisco

FOOD

Bloom
CHARLOTTE, N.C.

For Food Lion's new concept, Bloom, designers at api(+) began by defining what "convenience" means to today's shopper who barely has time to plan tonight's dinner. Such convenience starts at TableTop Circle, located at the front of the store and consisting of easy meal solutions, including Boston Market prepared foods and other take-home-and-eat items. The area also has a "Recipe of the Week" cold case where items for an entire recipe are grouped together. Computer screens located in this area and throughout grocery departments help shoppers locate products at the touch of the screen, and kiosks in the meat and wine departments offer recipes and party-planning tips.

Client | Food Lion Inc., Salisbury, N.C. – Robert Canipe; Tom Engelen; Robin Johnson, director, concept renewal-Bloom

Design/Architecture | api(+), Tampa, Fla. – Thomas Henken, design; Ryan Martin, environmental graphics; Raoul Baralt, architecture

Outside Design Consultant | CurtisAlan Partners LLC, Winnetka, Ill. (brand identity consultant)

General Contractor | Myers & Chapman, Salisbury, N.C.

Fixtures/Graphics Fabrication | Southeastern Products Inc., Greenville, S.C.

Wall and Floor Tile | Dal-Tile Corp., Tampa, Fla.

Flooring | Armstrong World Industries, Lancaster, Pa.

Lighting | Amerlux Intl. LLC, Appleton, Wis..

Refrigerated Cases | Kysor-WarrenColumbus, Ga.

Photography | Tim Buchman Photography, Charlotte, N.C.; Courtesy of Bloom, Charlotte, N.C.

Houlihan's
VARIOUS LOCATIONS
THROUGHOUT THE U.S.

Houlihan's, a popular classic American restaurant, wanted to incorporate highly customized music into its existing and future locations.

Audio/video solutions provider, PlayNetwork, collaborated with the restaurateur to develop richly customized programs that highlight the brand's unique traits and emotions – namely a stylish, casual restaurant and bar with an indie mentality, delivering on-trend drinks and contemporary-classic food. Music is assembled to suit the daily dining schedules and time of day. Each month, the eatery selects 30 songs from its current playlist to be known as the Houlihan's "H-List." Houlihan's even prints and inserts the H-List into its restaurant's menus and publishes its playlist on iTunes.

Client | Houlihan's Restaurants Inc., Leawood, Kan.
Audio/Video | PlayNetwork, Redmond, Wash.
Photography | Courtesy of Houlihan's Restaurants Inc., Leawood, Kan.

Seasonal

The holidays provide retailers a great opportunity to show off the best of the season. And while it's hard to believe that visual merchandisers continue to come up with imaginative, new ideas that often times outdo the previous year's presentation, they continue to cull from an endless supply of children's stories, fairy tales, current events and holiday traditions to create something truly magical.

Bloomingdale's New York windows were inspired by the film version of Andrew Lloyd Webber's hit musical, "The Phantom of the Opera," which was released in theaters in late 2004. Each window along Lexington Avenue featured one of six key scenes from the movie.

Nordstrom's 15 windows at its Seattle flagship featured over-scale chandeliers, crystal garlands, evergreen trees with ice crystals and large frosted roses.

In Neiman Marcus's downtown Dallas store, mannequins in each window were outfitted in couture fashion from past and current collections.

Bloomingdale's
NEW YORK

Bloomingdale's New York windows were inspired by the film version of Andrew Lloyd Webber's hit musical, "The Phantom of the Opera," which was released in theaters in late 2004.

Each window along Lexington Avenue featured one of six key scenes from the movie, including: "Masquerade," "Rooftop Lovers," "Hannibal Opera," "Within the Musical," "Christina's Dressing Room," "Gondola to Phantom's Lair" and "The Chandelier."

Design | Harry Medina, window director; Ed Sylvia, creative stylist; Joseph Cotugno, vp, visual merchandising

Props | Spaeth Design, New York; John McDevitt Metal Smithing, Brooklyn, N.Y.; Bloomingdale's Display Carpenter Shop, New York; David Duncan Antiques, New York; Newell Art Gallery, New York

Fabrics/Costumes | Militaryheritage.com, Manotick, Ont.; Viaggio Design, Farmingdale, N.Y.

Sculptured Arm Castings | Colbar Art, New York

Plasma Screen | Toshiba, Tokyo

Murals | Khuzami Studio, New York

Chandelier and Crystals | Swarovski, New York

Florals | Janette Rapp Floral Supply, Queens, N.Y.

Mannequins | Adel Rootstein Mannequins, New York

Architectural Elements | Elementsofhome.com, Chicago

Photography | Willo Font, New York

SEASONAL

Marshall Field's / Snow White

CHICAGO

Marshall Field's treated shoppers and tourists to a retelling of the popular children's story, "Snow White, the Fairest Tale of All."

Through a series of 11 window vignettes, the classic fairytale was told with a decidedly contemporary flair. Surrounded by a snow-kissed forest frame, the windows depicted Snow White from infancy to her friendship with the "seven little diamond miners" to her inevitable union with her handsome prince – and, of course, her battles with the very glamorous but evil queen determined to spoil her happiness. Charming details such as the queen's plasma screen 'magic mirror' and Snow White's Louis Vuitton-inspired bag delighted sharp-eyed viewers and gave the age-old story a more modern feel.

Design | Marshall Field's, Chicago – Jamie Becker, creative director; Amy Meadows, visual marketing manager
Animation/Window Sets | Spaeth Design, New York
Prosceniums | KINC, Chicago
Photography | Susan Kezon, Chicago

Neiman Marcus

DALLAS

For the 2004 holiday season, a custom 14-foot sugar tree composed of over one ton of sugar sparkled magically through Neiman Marcus's Palladian window in its downtown Dallas store. After much experimentation with sugar, the final product consisted of some 400 hard candy color disks, while 2000 delicate sugar ornaments floated through the center of the tree.

Glamour, luxury, holiday, whimsy and fantasy described the retailer's 10 additional windows. Mannequins in each window were outfitted in couture fashion from past and current collections. Implementing the Neiman Marcus icon, butterfly wings were constructed from the butterfly garland seen hanging in the atrium of many of its stores.

Design | Neiman Marcus downtown visual team, Dallas – Ignaz Gorischek, vp, visual planning and presentation; Bob White, visual manager; Ray Saunders, visual stylist

Custom Sugar Tree | Hanzon Studios, Denver

Photography | Zachary Stefaniak, Dallas

Tiffany & Co.
NEW YORK

Tiffany's holiday windows were full of jewels and the colorful illustrations that pop artist Andy Warhol created for Tiffany holiday greeting cards in the 1950s and 60s. The drawings appear in design director John Loring's new book, "Greetings from Andy (Warhol): Christmas at Tiffany's."

The windows highlighted Warhol's riotous ways with toys, ornaments, trees, doves and Santa's sleigh, with unexpected appearances by watermelon-snacking reindeer, a high-heeled red ankle boot stuffed with holly, mermaids and cherubs on a violin. The colorful displays also featured Warhol's diary entries, written at the bottom of the windows.

Design | Tiffany & Co., New York – Robert Rufino, vp of creative services and visual merchandising

Photography | Veronica Szarejko, New York

Burberry
NEW YORK

Burberry's two windows were designed as a fantasy transporting the passerby to an estate in the English countryside.

Trimmed boxwood hedges stood out against the blue sky and functioned as merchandising vehicles for various Burberry gift offerings. In addition to the hedges, one window featured a British couple with their dogs, while the other had the queen's guards marching behind the hedge.

Design | Burberry USA, New York – Sal Lenzo, vp, visual merchandising; Anthony Etienne, senior manager, visual, New York store; Glen Navarro, manager, visual, New York store; Cassey Cheesman, manager, visual, New York store

Background/Blue Mirror | Architectural Systems Inc., New York

Mannequins | Adel Rootstein Mannequins, New York

Hedges, Outdoor Hedge Garland on Exterior | American Christmas Decorations Inc., Bronx, N.Y.

Wooden Guards, Dogs | Ronis Brothers, Lynbrook, N.Y.

Photography | Zehavi and Cordes Photography, Brooklyn, N.Y.

Holt Renfrew
TORONTO

Holt Renfrew, the Toronto fashion retailer, chose "Fairytales" as its window theme, to reflect the magical aspect of the holidays and to celebrate the various stories' heroines.

Six windows represented the tales of Sleeping Beauty, Snow White, Little Red Riding Hood, Alice in Wonderland, Cinderella and the Princess and the Pea.

Designers used special-effect painting, abstract trees and realistic forest bedding to create detail and layering. Each heroine's gown was provided by the retailer's designer vendors, a key component in marrying the fairytale to the merchandise.

Design | Holt Renfrew, Toronto – Janis Bell, former national visual director; Mary Pompili, vp marketing; John Gerhardt, director of creative services; Tracey Peters, national visual merchandising manager; Susanne Shaw, window manager
Outside Design Consultant | Alison Koturbash, Toronto (set designer)
Set Building and Scenic Painting | LittleFeet, Toronto
Mannequins | Adel Rootstein Mannequins, New York
Florist | Forget-Me-Not Floral Design, Toronto
Photography | Jay Robinson, Saw Photography, Castleton, Ont.

Lord & Taylor
NEW YORK

Lord & Taylor's display windows celebrated the U.S. Postal Service's decades of commitment to delivering mail through snow, rain, heat and the gloom of night. Six animated windows were snapshots of the ways that the Postal Service has enabled people to stay connected over the years and how it brings joy to people's lives.

Each window chronicled a milestone in the history and development of the Postal Service by depicting modes of delivering mail – by horse, steamboat, stagecoach, steam locomotive, plane and truck.

Design | Lord & Taylor, New York – Manoel Renha, divisional vp, visual merchandising/fashion/special events; Barbara Smyth-Fitzgerald, fashion manager

Fabrication, Props, Animation, Scenic painting | Spaeth Design, New York

Special Occasion Dresses | Tim and Linda Platt, New York

Graphics | MMF Inc., New York

Research, Artwork, Props | U.S. Postal Service, Washington, D.C.

Wallpaper | Lee Jofa, Bethpage, New York

Graphics/Lightboxes | Expotrans Inc., Lake Forest, Calif.

Lighting Components | Barbizon, New York

Props/Decorations | Roman Inc., Roselle, Ill.; Autograph Foliages, Cleveland; Salzburg Creations, Bronx, N.Y.; Superior Studios, Commerce, Calif.; Aldik, Moorpark, Calif.; Dept. 56, New York

Photography | Richard Cadan, Brooklyn, N.Y.

Furniture and Accessories

Bergdorf Goodman
NEW YORK

Bergdorf Goodman composed each of its windows around a famous phrase chosen to evoke emotions and sentiments associated with the season. Quotations were taken from such sources as William Shakespeare, Salvador Dali, Plato, Italo Calvino and Lewis Caroll.

Each quote – appearing framed in the window – acted as a doorway to an elaborate fantasy, with layers of meanings and allusions. And, in keeping with Bergdorf's customary approach, each window was completely different. One window, celebrating overindulgence, had figurines covered in chocolate surrounded by cakes and all manner of chocolate edibles, while another had a giant white peacock and women dressed in white furs decked in jewelry and surrounded by crystals hanging from branches overhead.

Design | Bergdorf Goodman, New York – Linda Fargo, vp, visual merchandising; David Hoey, window director; Bergdorf Goodman display staff

Photography | Zehavi and Cordes Photography, Brooklyn, N.Y.

Nordstrom

SEATTLE

Nordstrom's 15 windows at its Seattle flagship featured over-scale chandeliers, crystal garlands, evergreen trees with ice crystals and large frosted roses for the theme of "Wishing You a Season of Surprise and Delight."

Design | Nordstrom Visual Merchandising Flagship Team, Seattle
Photography | Alan Abramowitz, Seattle

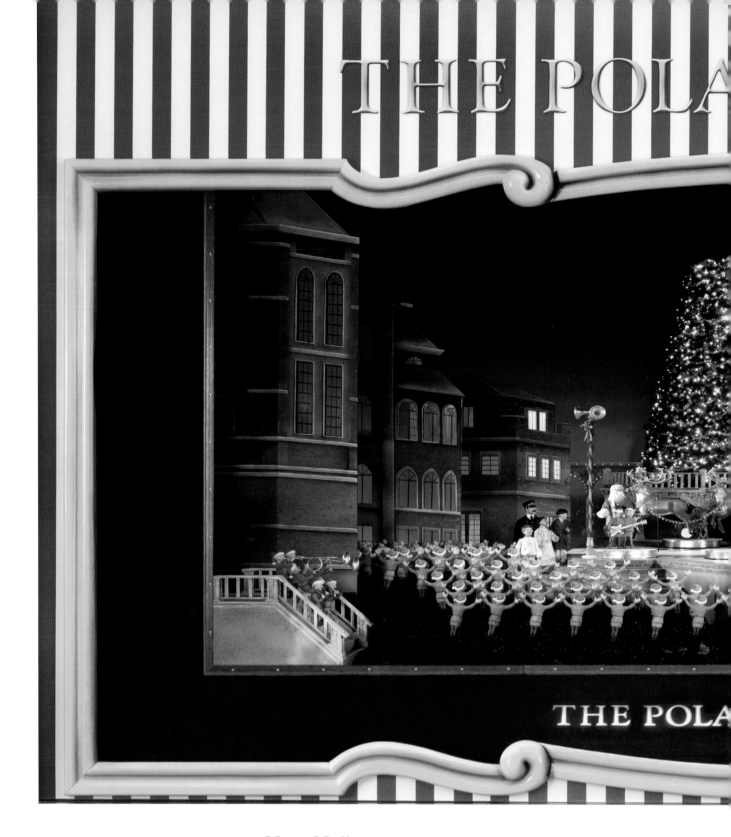

THE POLA

THE POLA

Myer Melbourne

MELBOURNE, AUSTRALIA

Myer Melbourne's six holiday windows depicted scenes from *The Polar Express*, based upon the book written and illustrated by Chris Van Allsburg and inspired by images from the Warner Bros. movie.

Client | Myer Ltd. – Myer Melbourne Department Store, Melborne, Australia; Paul Bonnici, director, marketing and creative

Design and Construction | Stage One Promotions Pty. Ltd., Port Melbourne, Australia – John Kerr, creative director

Photography | Rob Anderson, South Yarra, Australia

All Through the Night

Everyone tries out their own idea to get the melting task done.
Star uses her glasses as a magnifying prism by holding them up to the sun.

Todos proponen fabulosas ideas para descongelar el trineo inmediatamente
Con ayuda del sol, aunque no lo creas. Estrella hace una lupa de sus lentes.

Sears
CHICAGO

Designers at Sears wrote and illustrated an original holiday story for its windows, entitled "The Great Big Snow." The story is told over a span of 15 windows about two young mice children who help Santa overcome a giant snow storm that is preventing him from delivering holiday gifts. Colorful graphics and text (in both English and Spanish) accompanied the windows.

Design | Sears in-house design team, Chicago – Glenn Russell, senior design director; Tom Baldoni, illustrator; Lois Rafinksi, administrative

Sets and Animation | Set Piece Productions, West Dundee, Ill., Bill Cwiklinski, Karen Cwiklinksi, Sue Rachke, Tony LaGrassa

Lights and Lasers | ProSand Audio, Los Angeles

Vertical Motion Conveyors | Joliet Pattern, Crest Hill, Ill.

Photography | Glenn Russell, Chicago

House of Fraser
LONDON

House of Fraser created stylish windows using layers of white, frosted and sparkling paper, while curvaceous shelves elevated the
mannequins that were surrounded by paper
garlands to create a winter wonderland.

Design | House of Fraser in-house design, London – Helen
Curtis, creative design controller, Annika Jeffries, creative design
coordinator, Julia Cronk, creative design manager, Jamie Shouli,
visual manager
Scheme | Artefacts, Kent, U.K.
Mannequins | Bonaveri, London
Photography | Melvin Vincent, Spotlight Studios, London